THE PRECEDENT.:
(PROVISION CHRONICLES.)

DWIGHT DRUMMOND

Ordering Information:

For orders and inquiries, please contact:
1-888-404-1388
www.goldtouchpress.com
book.orders@goldtouchpress.com

Printed in the United States of America

CONTENTS

THE PRECEDENT:
(PROVISION CHRONICLES.)

Preface: The Precedent: (Provision Chronicles) exemplify the importance of monetary clemency.

Description: The Precedent: (Provision Chronicles) amplify the importance of monetary clemency.

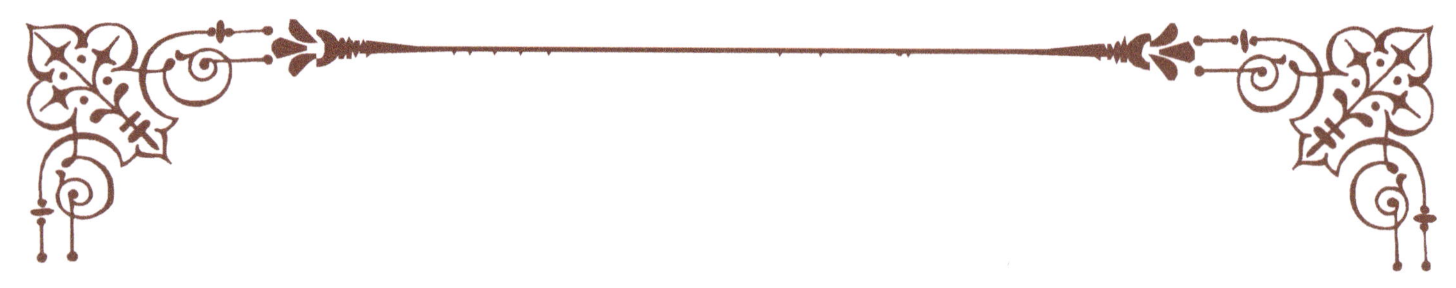

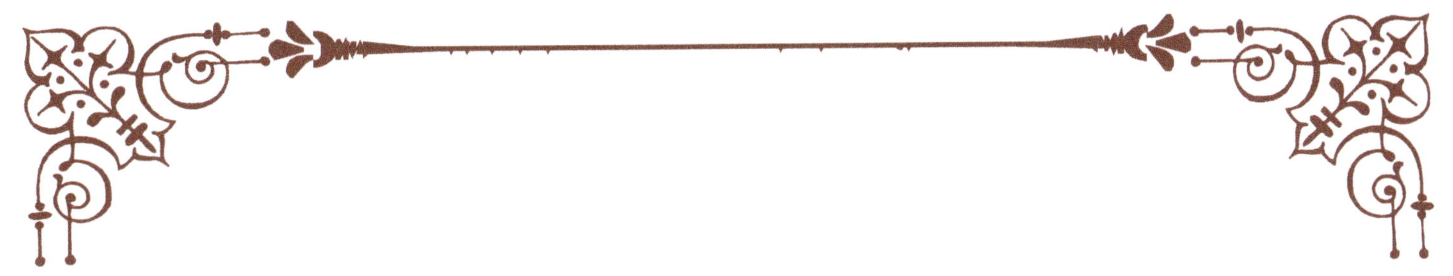

Love without Prendergast.

Even In separation I see it every need to wonder about this woman. I seek to Understand but never seem to know how important she is toward the likes of calling her my own............."

"Love without Prendergast."

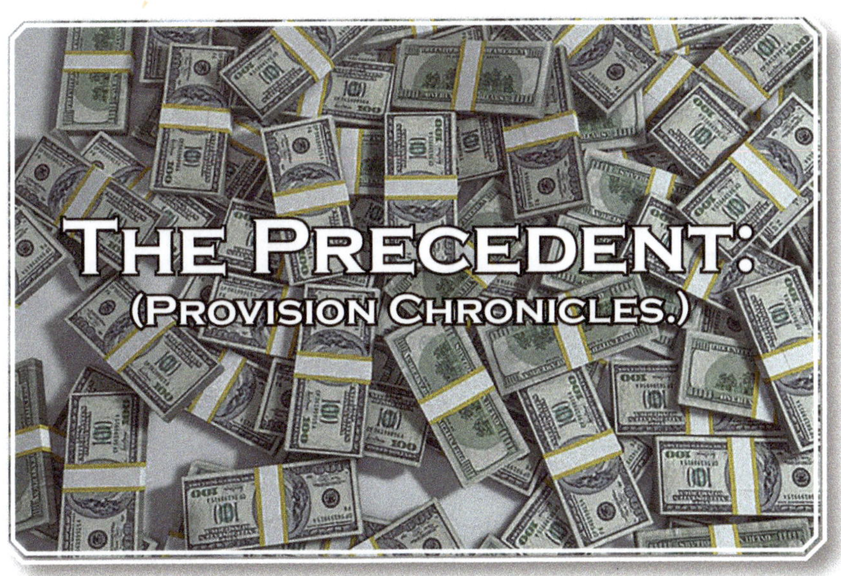
THE PRECEDENT:
(PROVISION CHRONICLES.)

The Prendergast

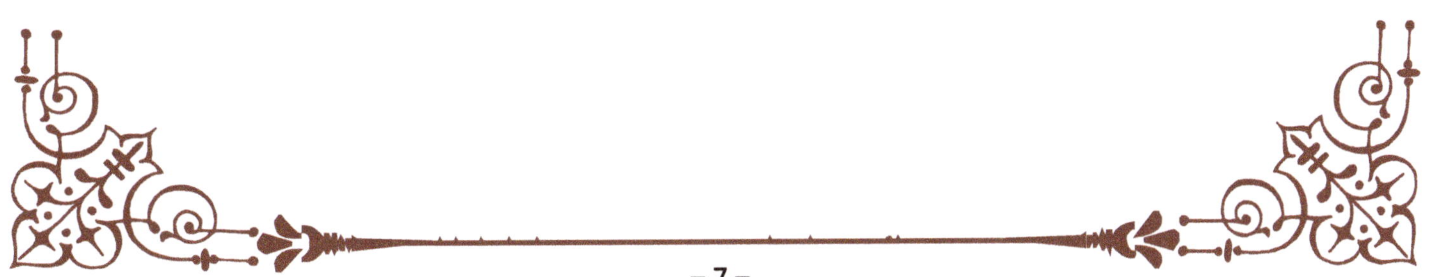

As a Man I don't understand you as a woman;
though we may see each other as we trod on the same path toward
Life. I'm not angry with you but disappointed against the fact that I
don't have the right to love you,
In that moment of time............."

"The Prendergast."

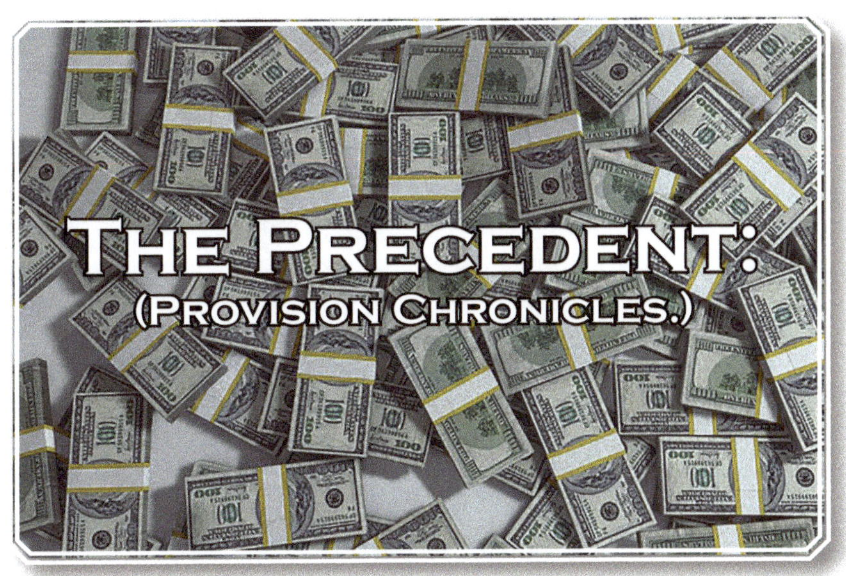
THE PRECEDENT:
(PROVISION CHRONICLES.)

Bobfest

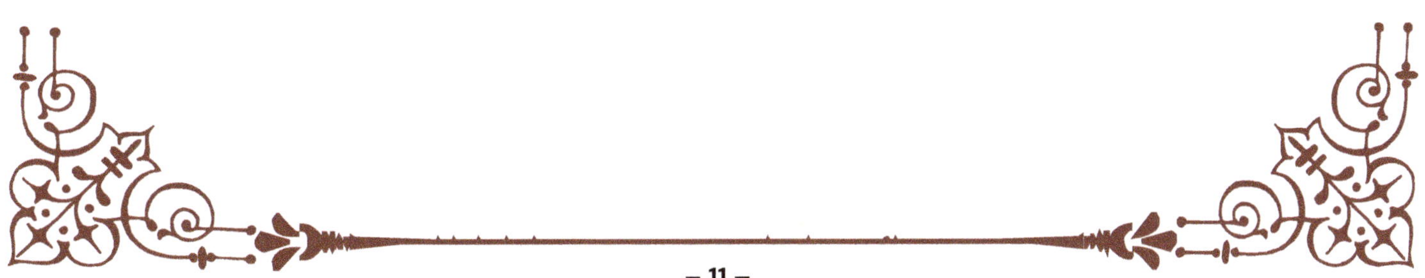

In celebration of a Reggae icon that captivated the attention of
Millions around the Globe and cause the People in Jamaica to
be United with Peace for a Political cause is the reason why I say
Bobfest....................."

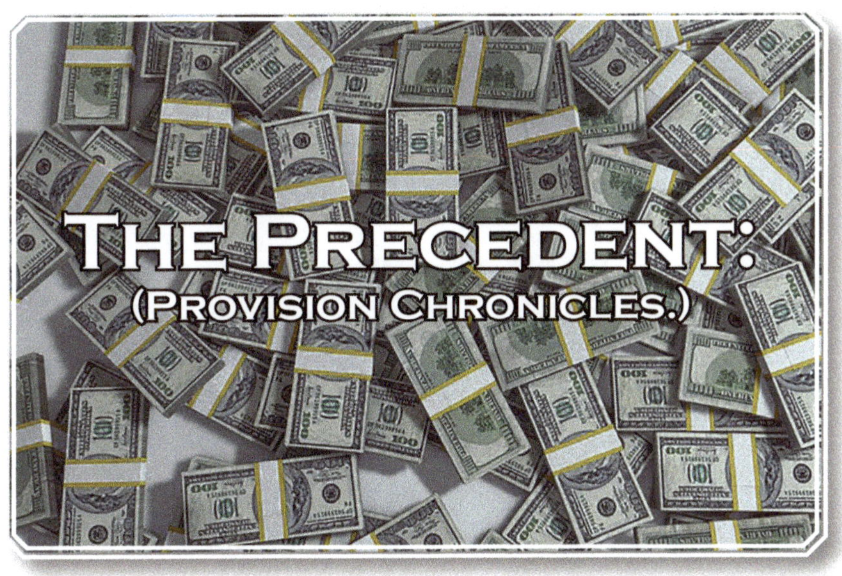

THE PRECEDENT:
(PROVISION CHRONICLES.)

D. DRUMMOND.

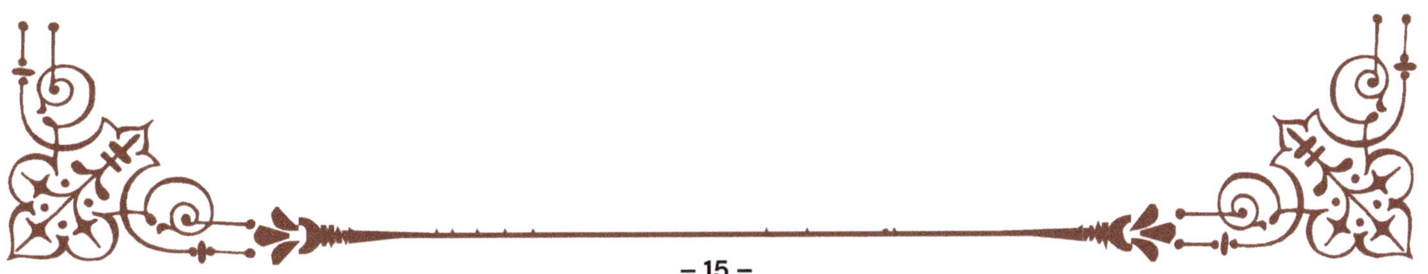

A Poet captivated by the likes of Literary notions that set the theater
of dramatic tales written in slowly detailed gestures from a man
D. Drummond.

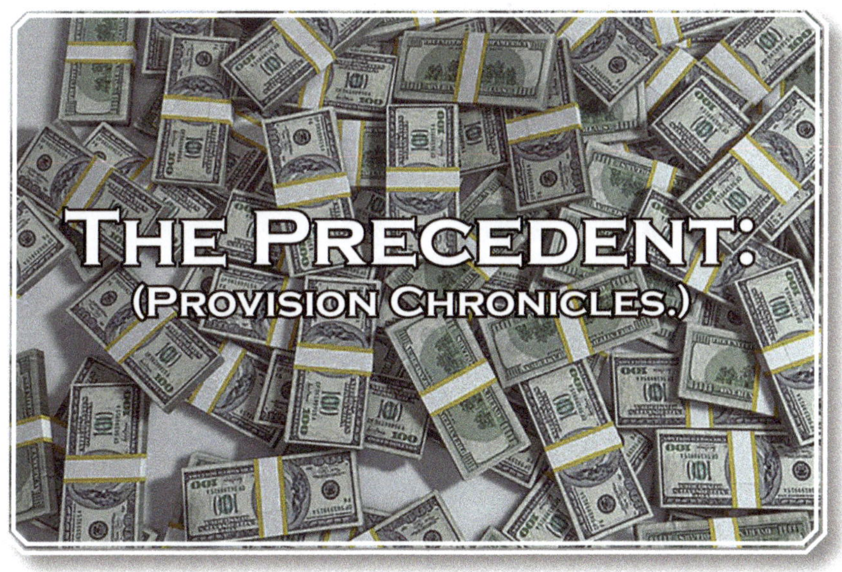

THE PRECEDENT:
(PROVISION CHRONICLES.)

'THE KING'

13 MASSIVE HITS FROM THE PAST

FEATURING:
DEAREST
DR. DECKER
FEELING FINE
GARDEN OF LOVE
KNOCK OUT PUNCH
LATIN GOES SKA
OCCUPATION
SILVER DOLLAR
STREET CORNER
WOMAN A COME...

DON DRUMMOND

DRUMFEST.

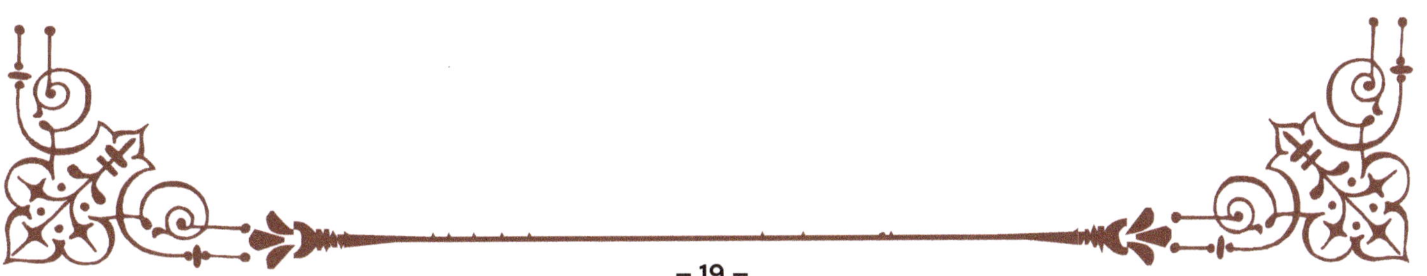

In celebration of a ska genius that captivated the world with his own trombone Don Drummond a man that was highly revered but deeply troubled by the acts of Life call trails and tribulations that we must get over as all remember him when we celebrate at Drumfest…………."

The Precedent:
(Provision Chronicles.)

VALERIE
JUNE
PUSHIN'
AGAINST
A STONE

OH! JUNE.

Her words are like gumbo it soothes the soul from pain and irritation
is the need for Music. We celebrate this Black but folk country music
Artist. I'd listen to get music whenever I feel the need to not be myself.

"Oh! June."

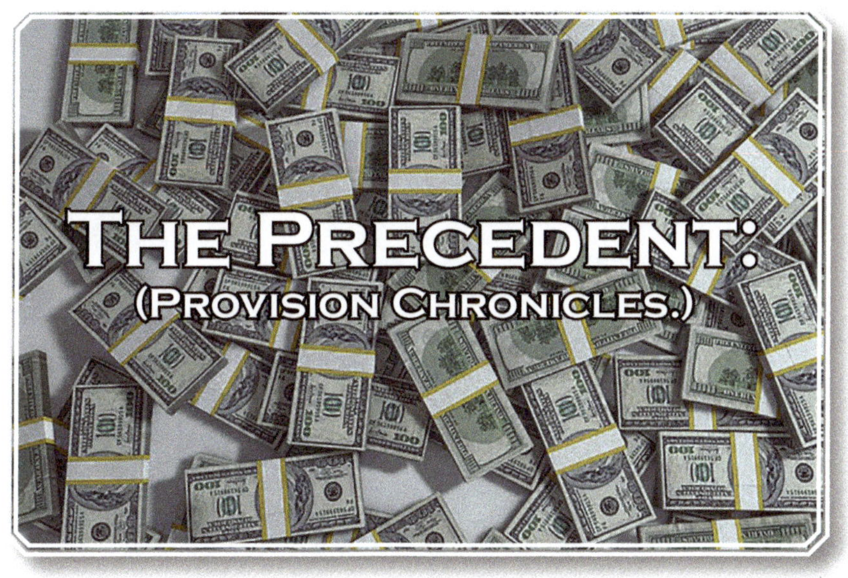

THE PRECEDENT:
(PROVISION CHRONICLES.)

DRUMMOND EATS.

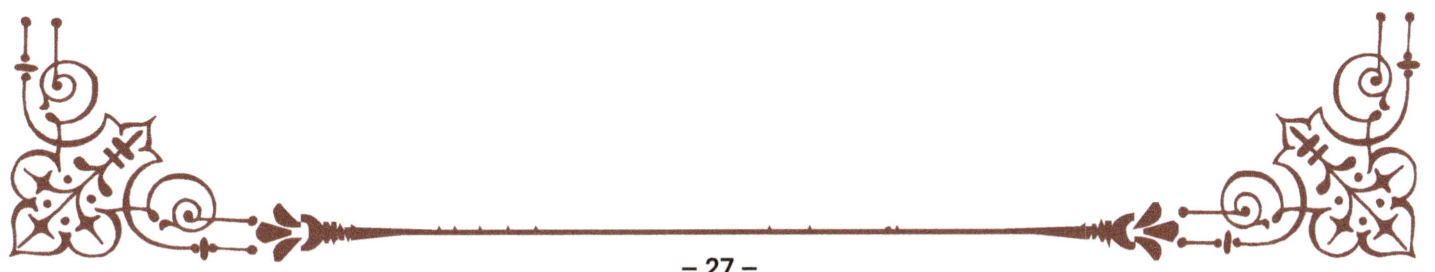

Even in distress success isn't the cause of stress but the whereabouts
in feast we Drummond Eats………….."

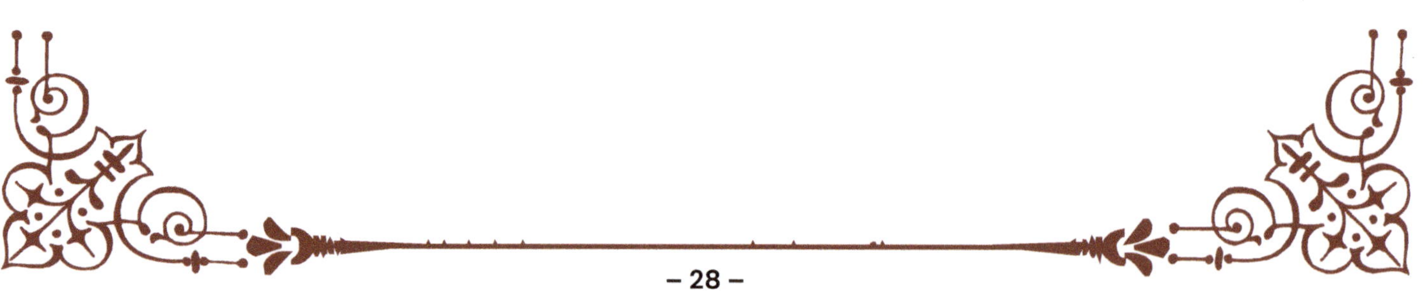

THE PRECEDENT:
(PROVISION CHRONICLES.)

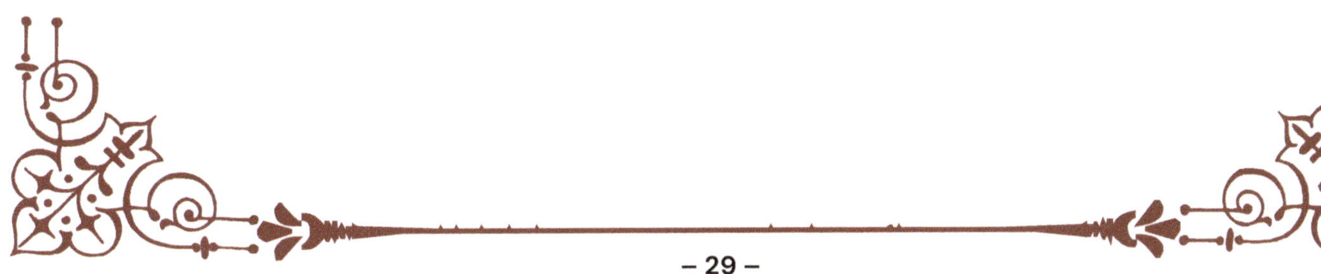

STUDIO 1
DON DRUMMOND
DON DRUMMOND
DON COSMIC
ROLL ON SWEET DON
DON COSMIC
COOLIE BOY
SURPLUS
THE SHOCK
SCHOOLING THE DUKE
RELOAD
LAST CALL TAKE 1
LAST CALL TAKE 2
FAR EAST
GREEN ISLAND
JET STREAM
THE ROCKET
SCRAP IRON
RAIN OR SHINE 1
RAIN OR SHINE 2
RAIN OR SHINE 3
GROOVING WITH THE BEAT
SERENADE IN SOUND
S1004
STUDIO 1

Drummond not Drummond.

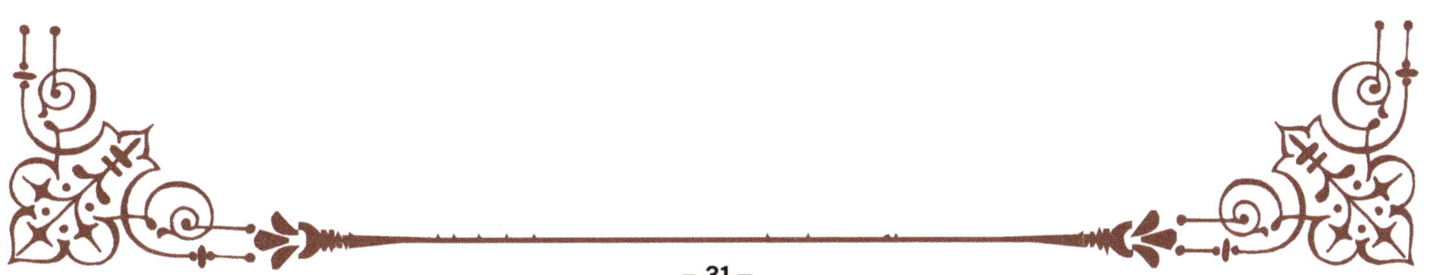

Drummond isn't the name you can easily use to protect yourself from intruders that seek to steal who we are for themselves. Every Drummond possess their own talent of success we hold individually but Understand that I am Dwight Drummond not Drummond................"

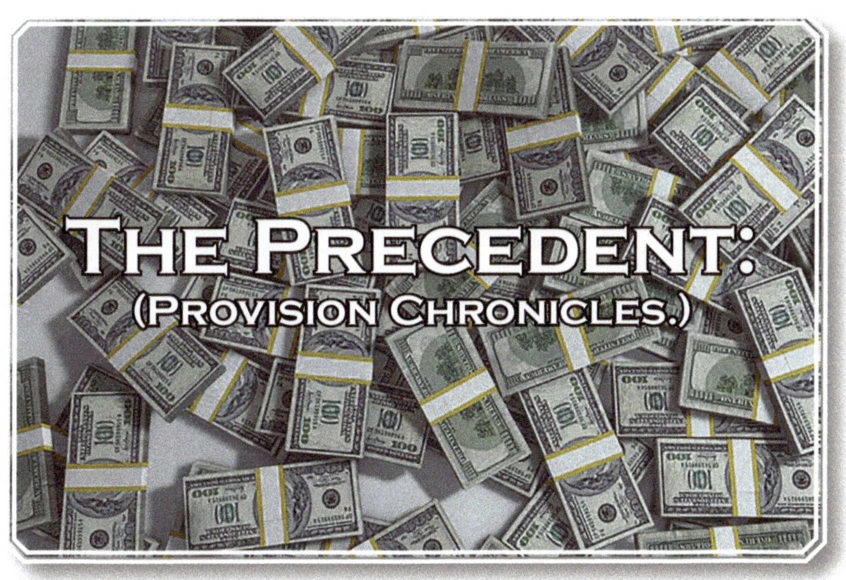
THE PRECEDENT:
(PROVISION CHRONICLES.)

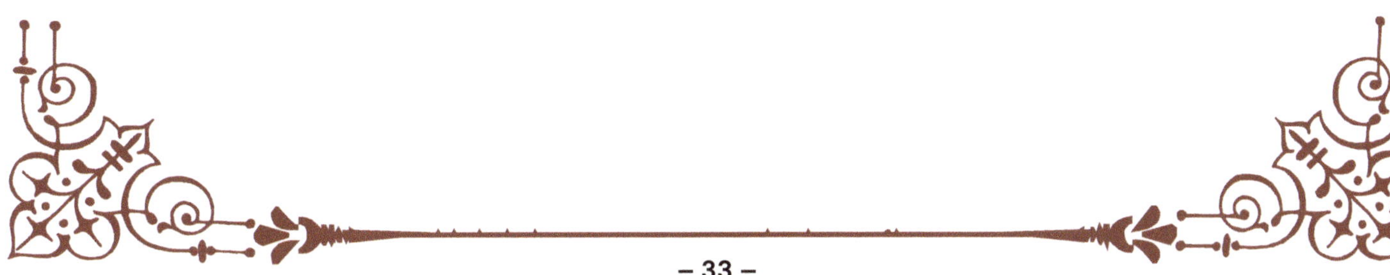

WHEN GOD SAY NO!

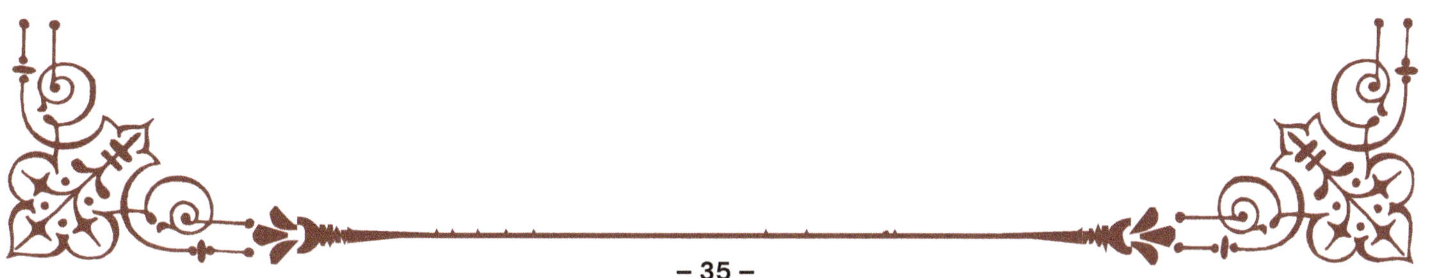

When Godly Inspirations leads to the fact of public recognition see it recommendable in exploitation to be yourself even with corruption which causes people toward change stay the same................"

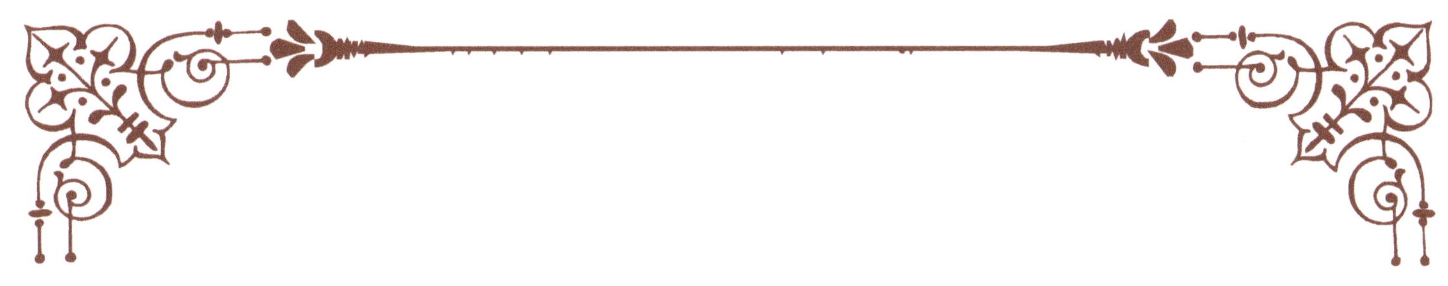

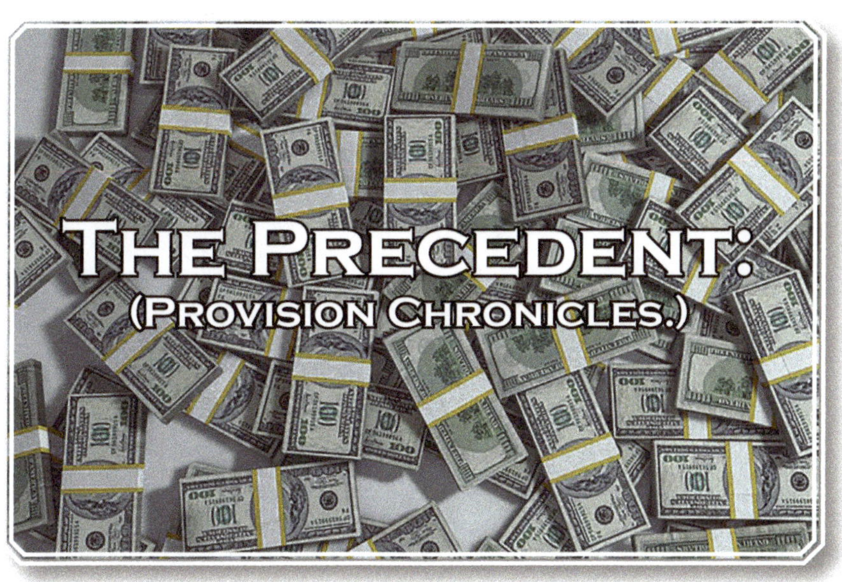

The Precedent:
(Provision Chronicles.)

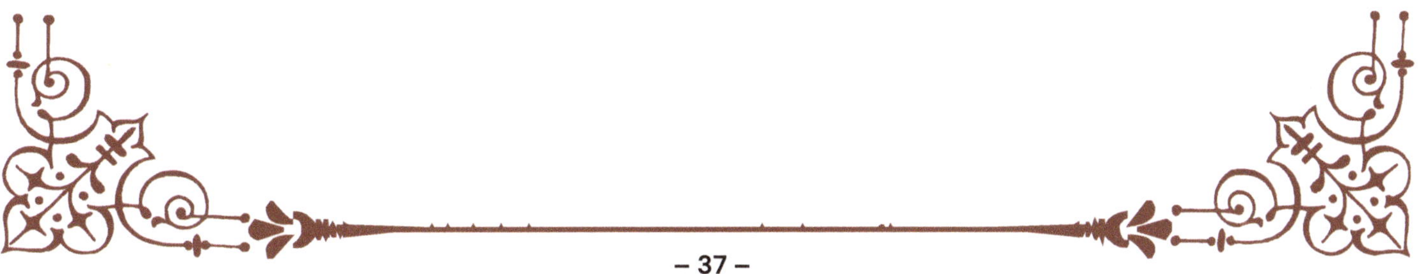

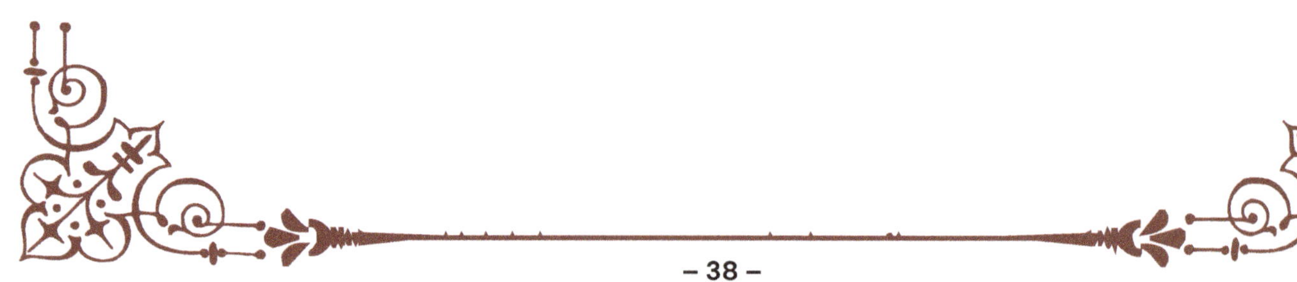

BEEFEST.

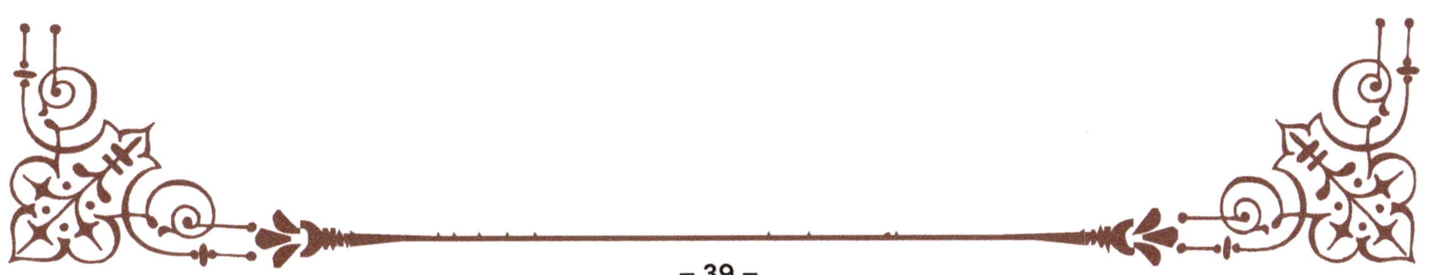

A Legendary Artist but Rasta his every voice nobody knows but everybody care about this Grammy award winner. The acts for his accomplishments soothes women alike around the globe but people are in a uproar at Beefest..........."

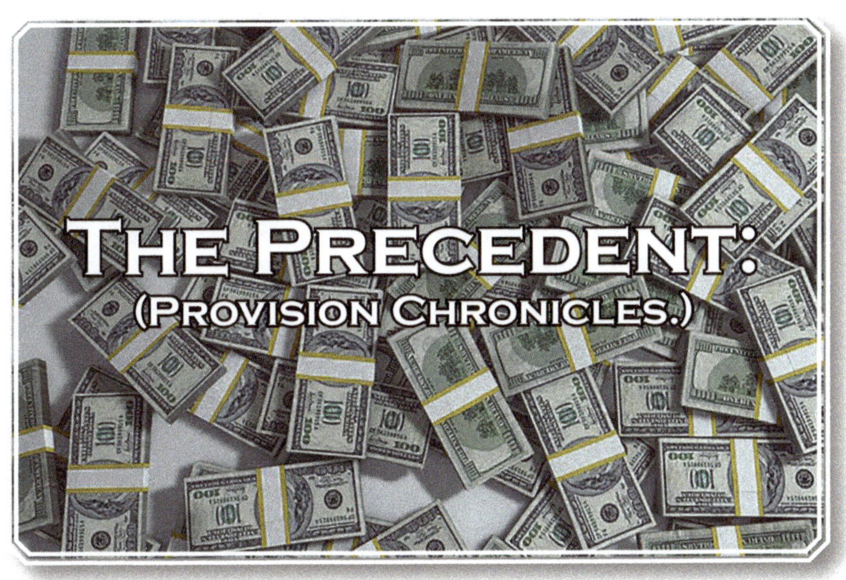

THE PRECEDENT:
(PROVISION CHRONICLES.)

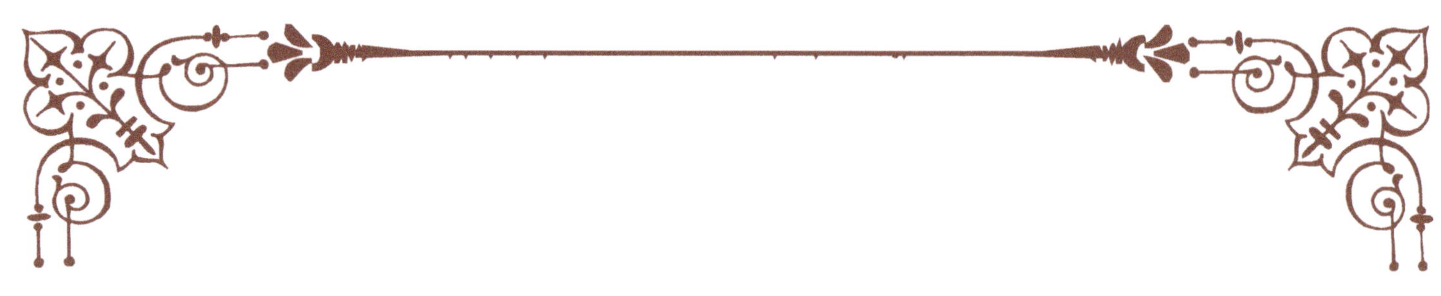

Alkafest.

In celebration we celebrate the most downloaded Dancehall
Artist highly revered and mostly talked about as
people wonder and stare it's Alkaline........................"

"Alkafest."

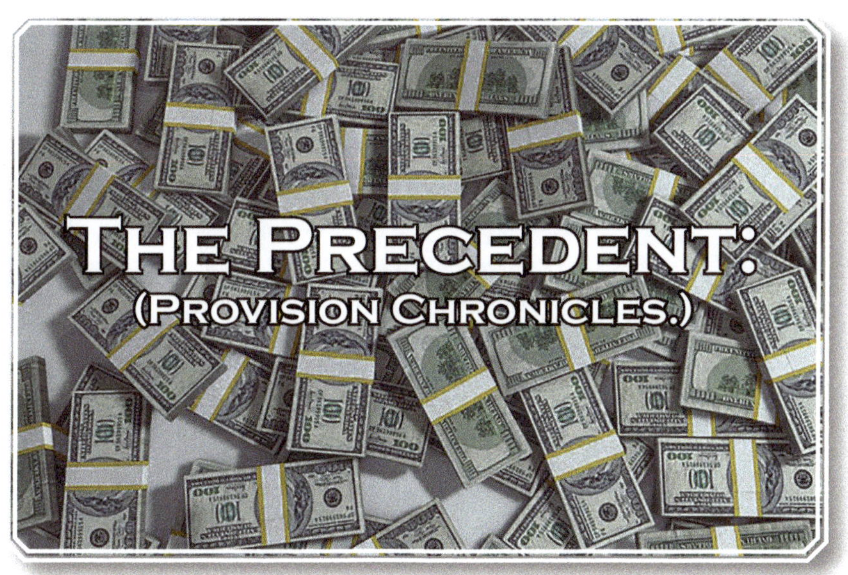

THE PRECEDENT:
(PROVISION CHRONICLES.)

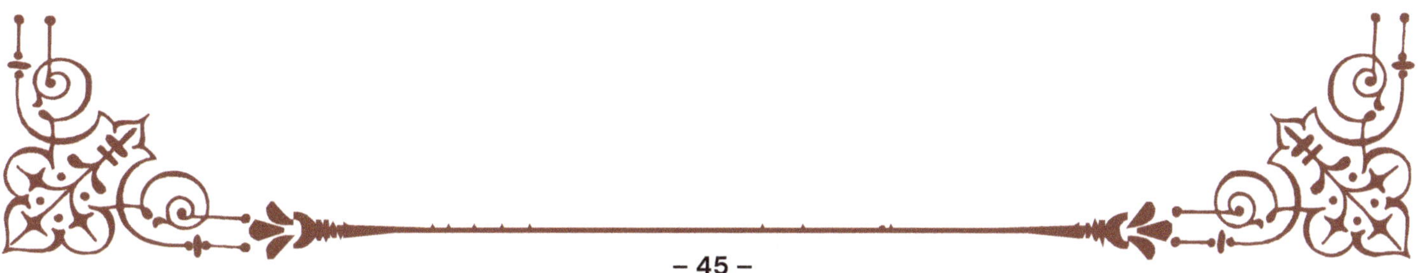

Mercedes-Maybach

Maybach.

A Mercedes Benz highly priced with the double mark of monetary
monopoly see it necessary to even help those less fortunate
People in low class neighborhoods before you go out and
buy a Maybach.

THE PRECEDENT:
(PROVISION CHRONICLES.)

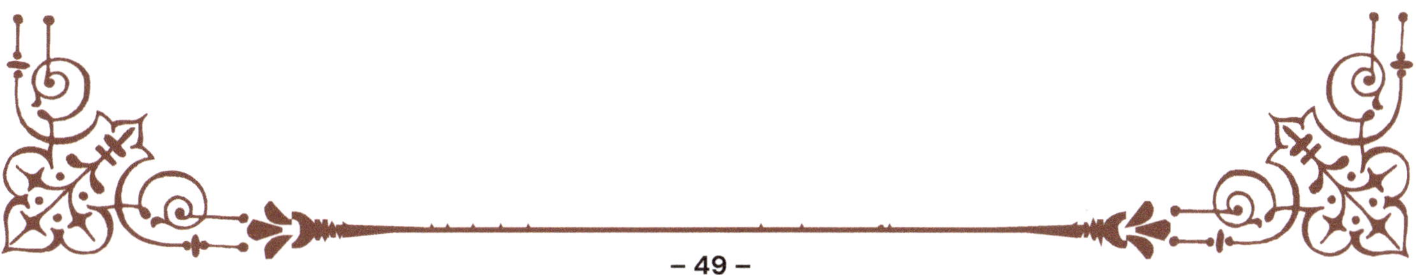

Prendergast and Presence.

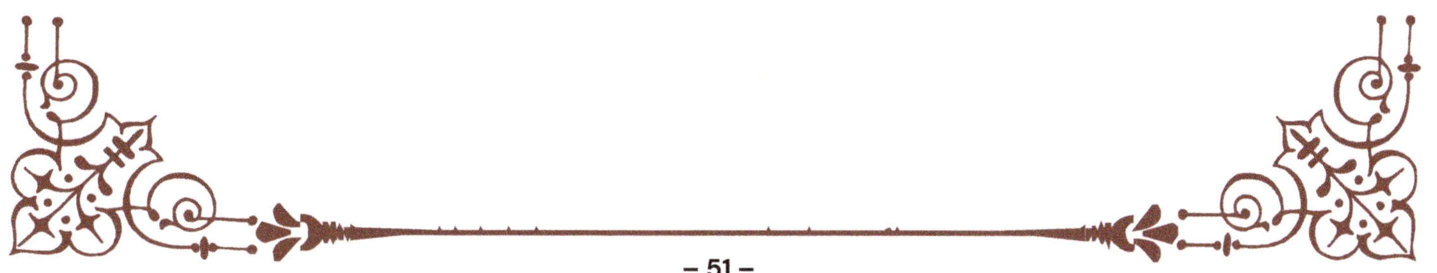

Ms. Prendergast is a woman that represents the prestige of a Rasta Cleopatra which uses her intellect to inspire those driven toward knowledge for who the Majesty in Haile Selassie truly is but even though I honor her not just as a Queen Menen which represents the class of a Black woman with Presence…………"

THE PRECEDENT:
(PROVISION CHRONICLES.)

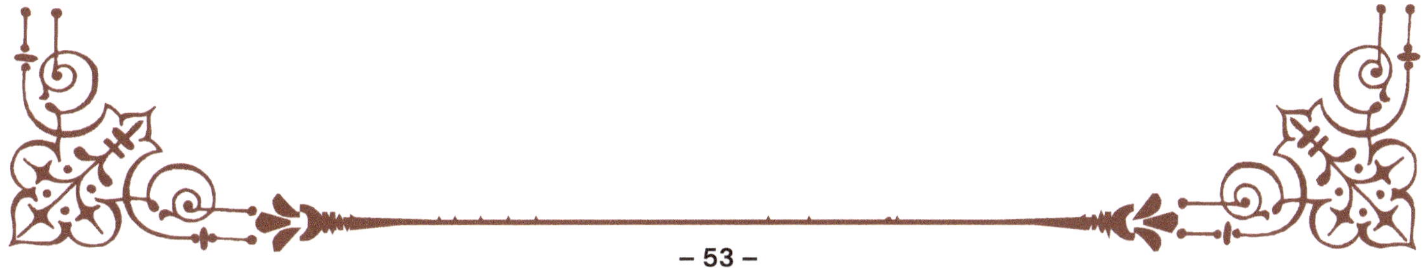

"The Phone."

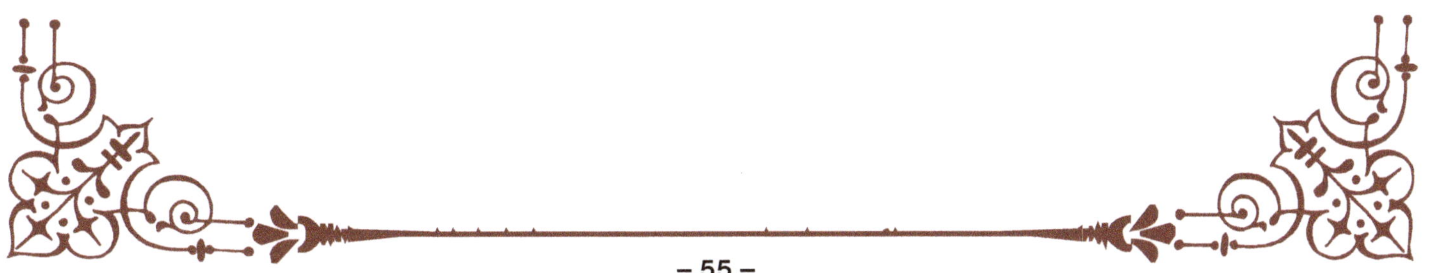

Though hidden from acknowledgement of a woman. I do see it possible to even make one call on "The Phone."

THE PRECEDENT:
(PROVISION CHRONICLES.)

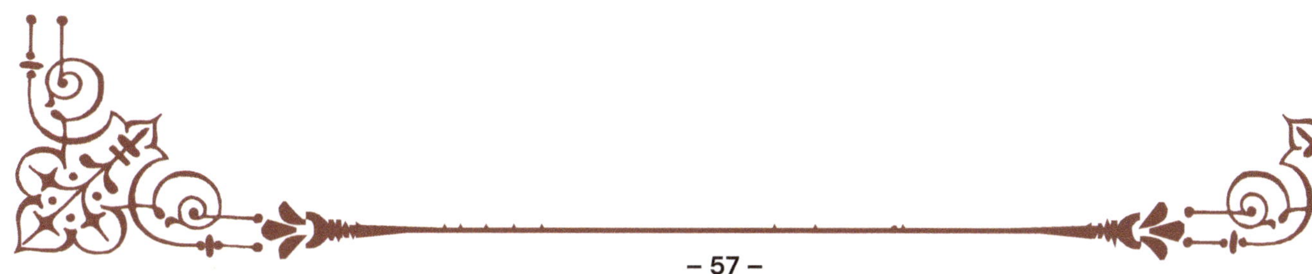

Police & Policy.

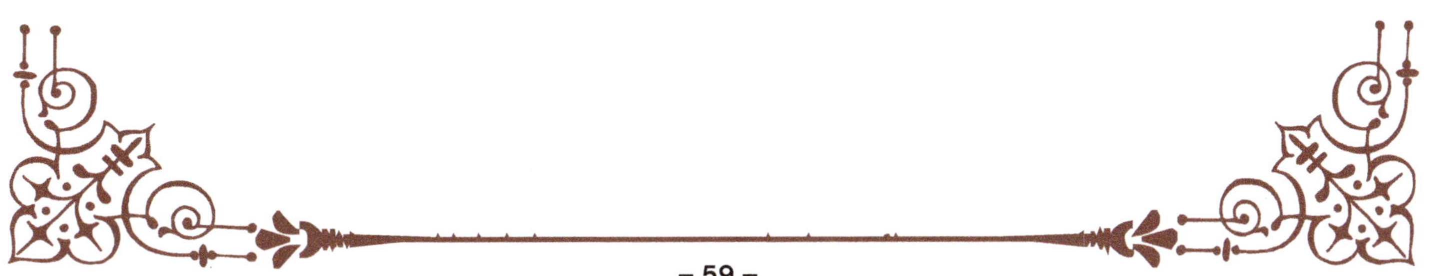

In this moment we must take action against undignified Police officers.
Who use their force of Protection as a will to misrepresent;
the conduct for freewill People in living their lives to
Love one to another as normal citizens again.

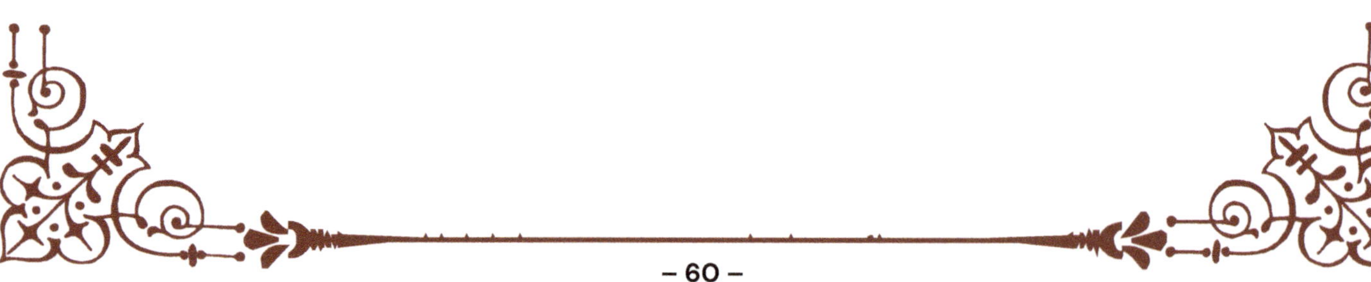

THE PRECEDENT:
(PROVISION CHRONICLES.)

MIGHT CANNOT DEFEAT RIGHT!
#OCCUPYPINNACLE

Prendergast Activism.

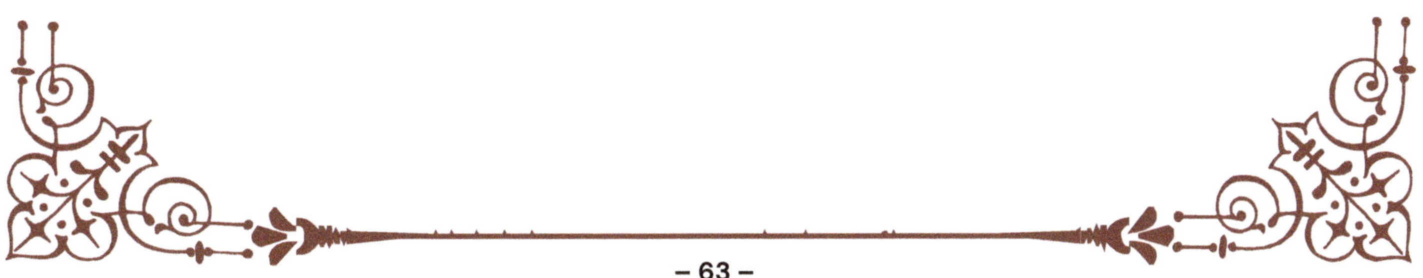

Not Malcolm X, Not Martin Luther King, but Donisha is a woman that pushes the status quo of Rastafari to the masses in a righteous way of simplicity and reality from the point of view standpoint with humility I speak about Prendergast Activism................"

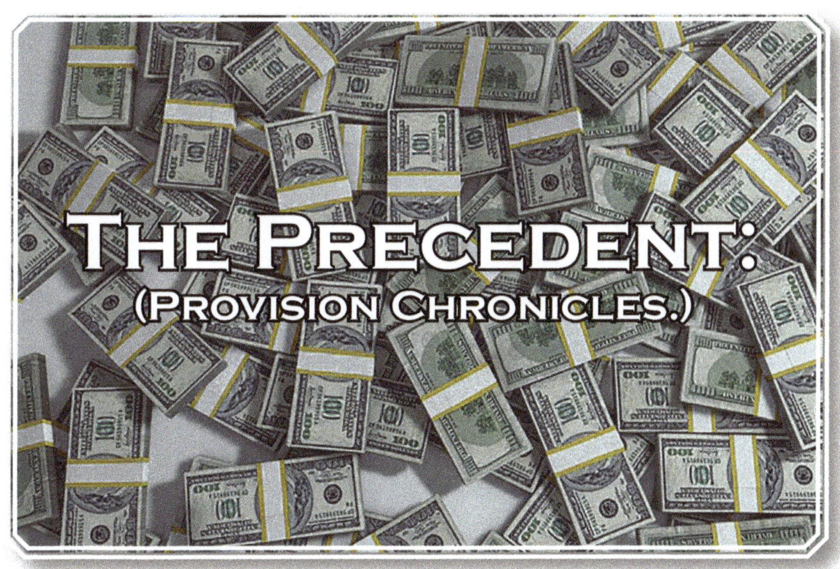

THE PRECEDENT:
(PROVISION CHRONICLES.)

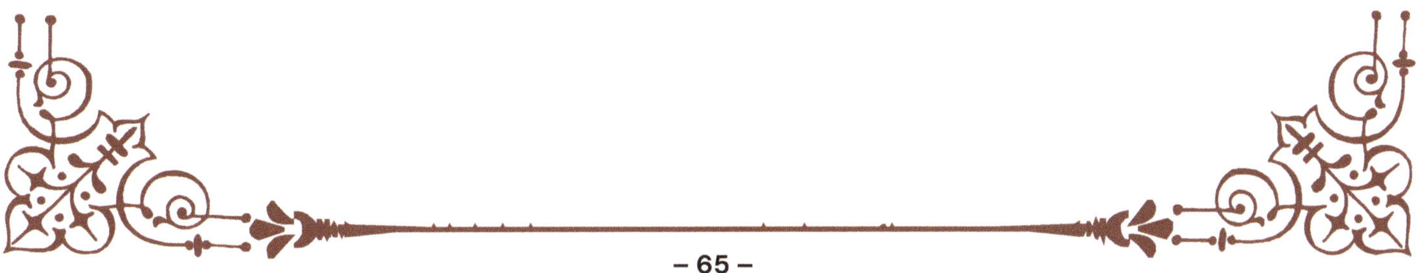

DRUMMOND ON THE INTERNET.

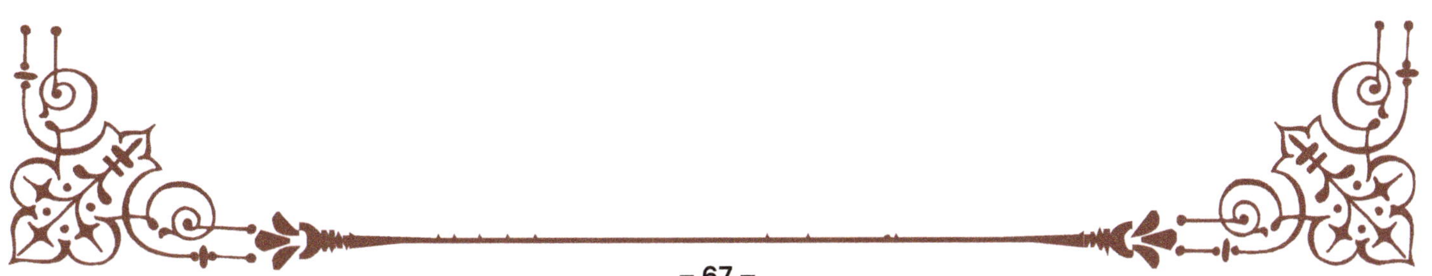

Even In exploitation of thy artistry just see it necessary to push forward with every word toward success that they hate to express but seek to stress that isn't important in understanding is Dwight Drummond on the Internet................"

"Drummond on the Internet."

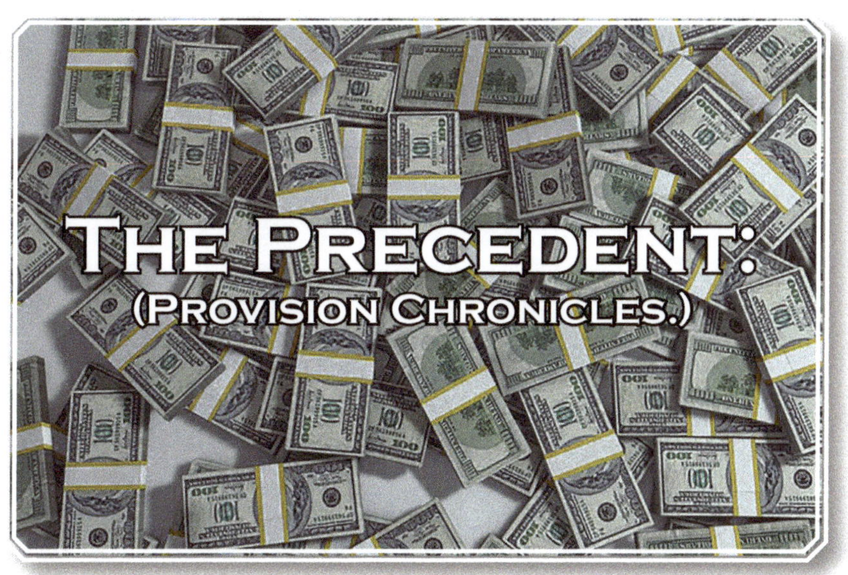
THE PRECEDENT:
(PROVISION CHRONICLES.)

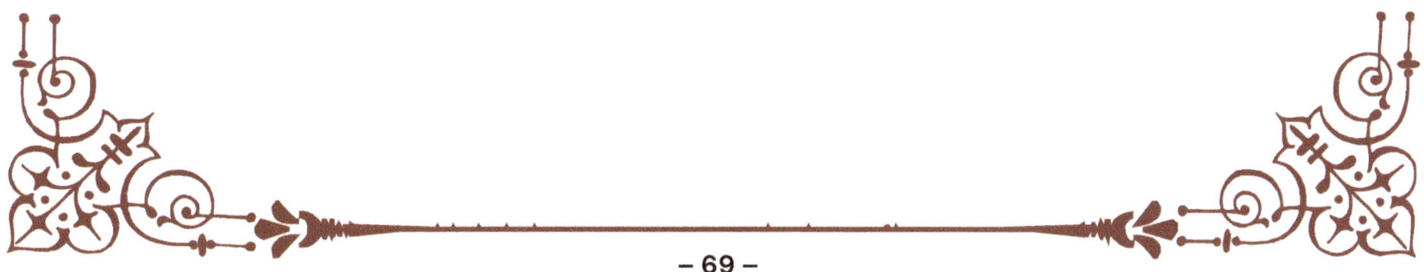

SADE.

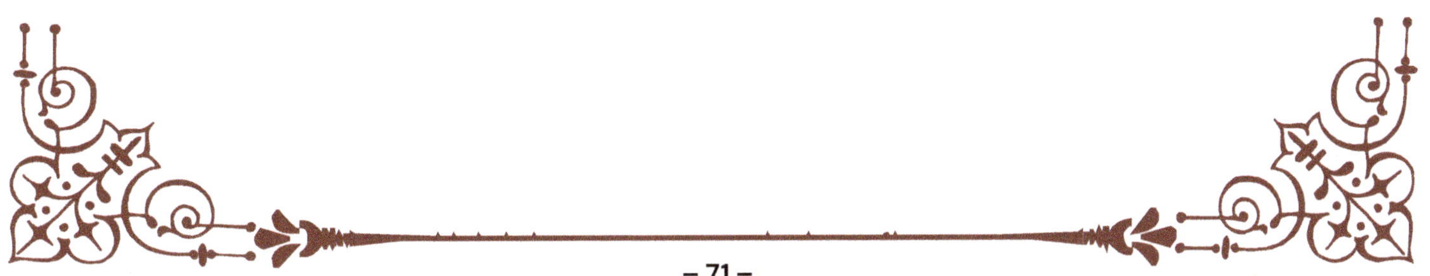

Her Love is Queen yet the importance of such woman shouldn't be
mention in deed but songs as we sing along "Sade."

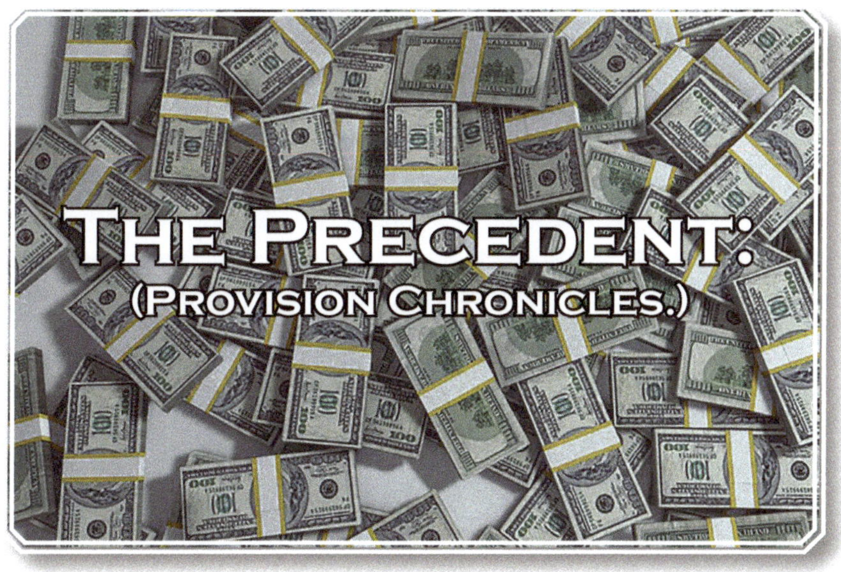
THE PRECEDENT:
(PROVISION CHRONICLES.)

Sapphire & Swiss.

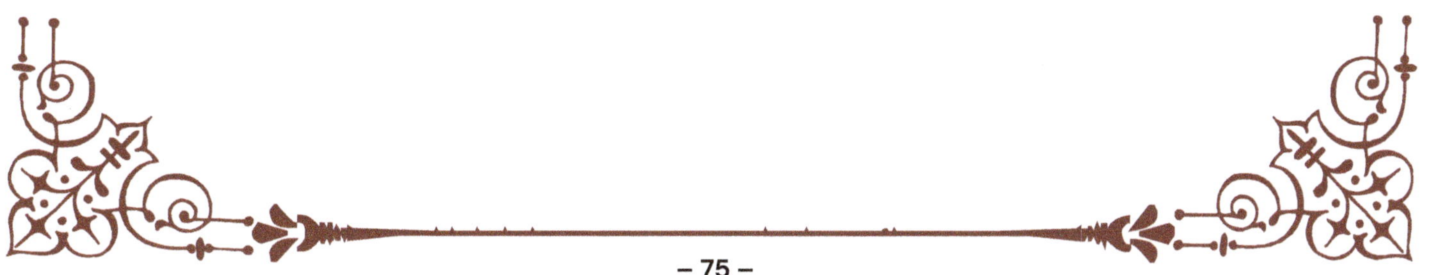

A Sapphire isn't a Diamond but a reliable source of importance
which is attached to foreign attire we call Swiss.

THE PRECEDENT:
(PROVISION CHRONICLES.)

SYKA.

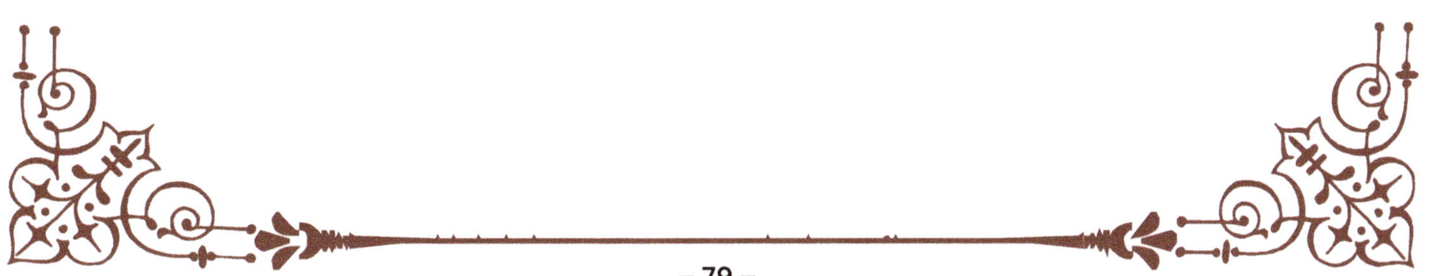

Syka isn't' the origination of Ska music but the new age in sound we call foreign Jamaican appeal for generation onward.............."

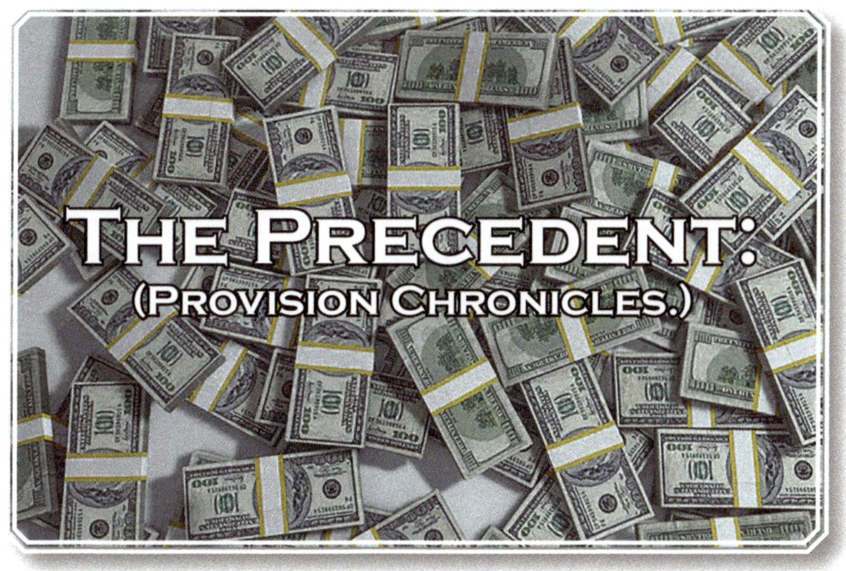
The Precedent:
(Provision Chronicles.)

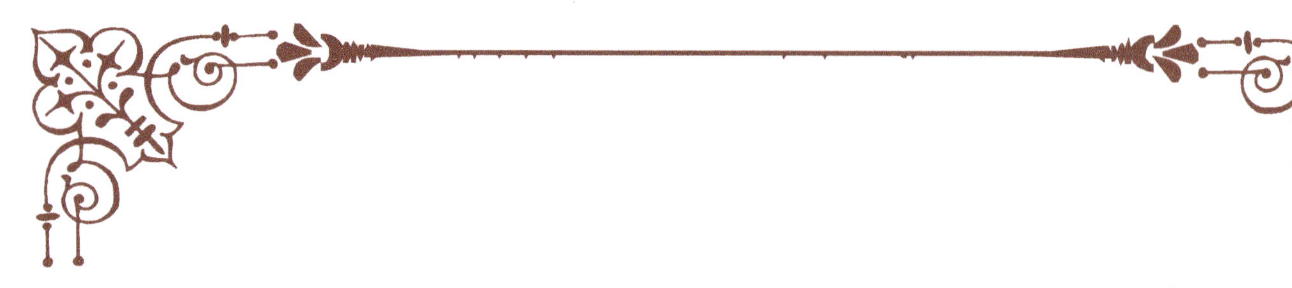

RUNNING THE DRUMMOND.

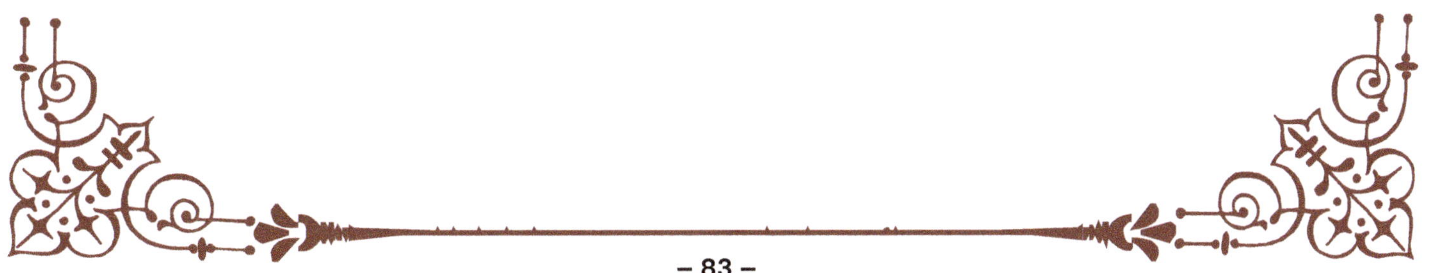

There are many relatives who see the success of Drummond as a plough to railroad; the importance in commitment of honor and respect. Though I don't broadcast my accomplishments openly to override the reality of Life. I see at times that there is no way but to runaway some people who call themselves Drummond.............."

THE PRECEDENT:
(PROVISION CHRONICLES.)

LITERARY TREATY.

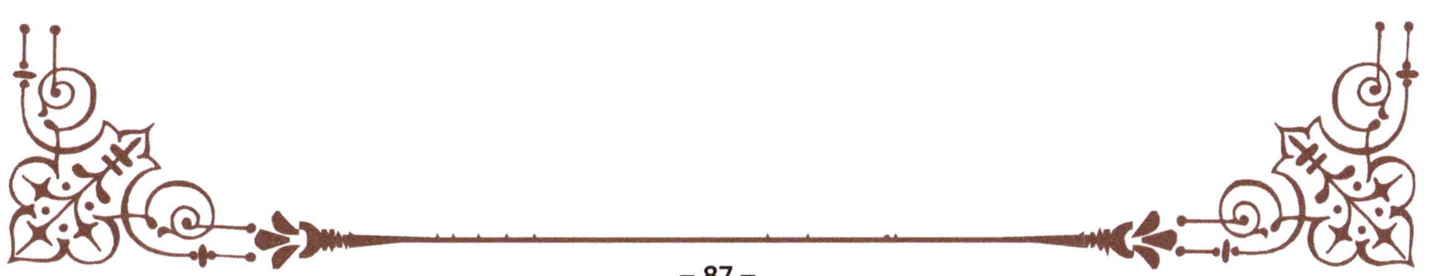

We were destined from Ancestry to be United in Matrimony. The Love
I have for you isn't public but sacred. When I see the reality of your
beauty. I know that you are a Queen but you must also know that
a King should require respect. regardless of the situation; we must
come together and be one with a Literary treaty not just Rasta but
predictable and personal for People.

THE PRECEDENT:
(PROVISION CHRONICLES.)

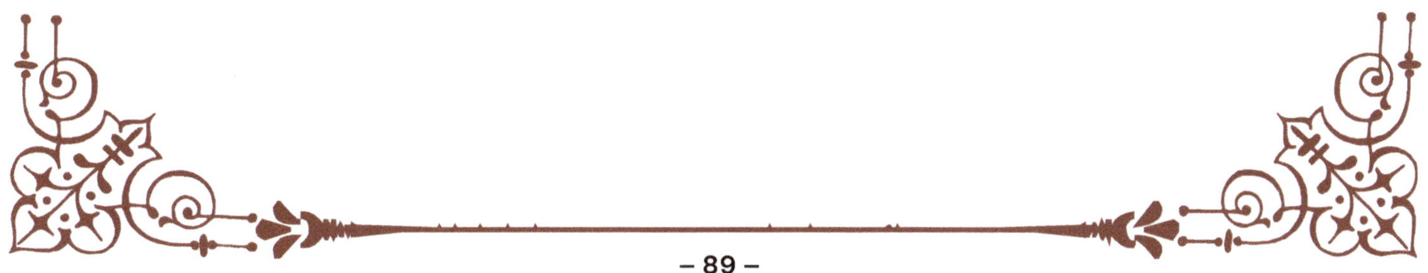

HEIGHT ABOVE
SEA LEVEL
1305 FEET
KINGSTON
TICKETS

NEW KINGSTON.

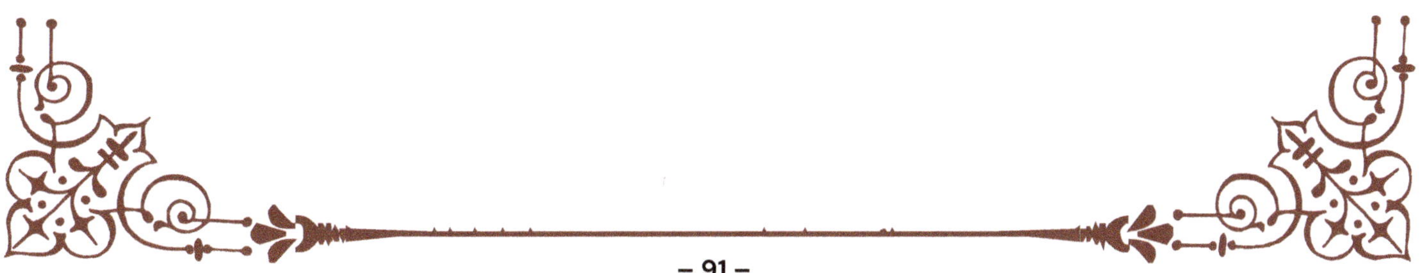

New Kingston where Business dialogue is the daily issue Life as usual is overloaded by times which causes the right for strife where the less fortunate is overlook because of their pay braket.

THE PRECEDENT:
(PROVISION CHRONICLES.)

10TH DOLLAR

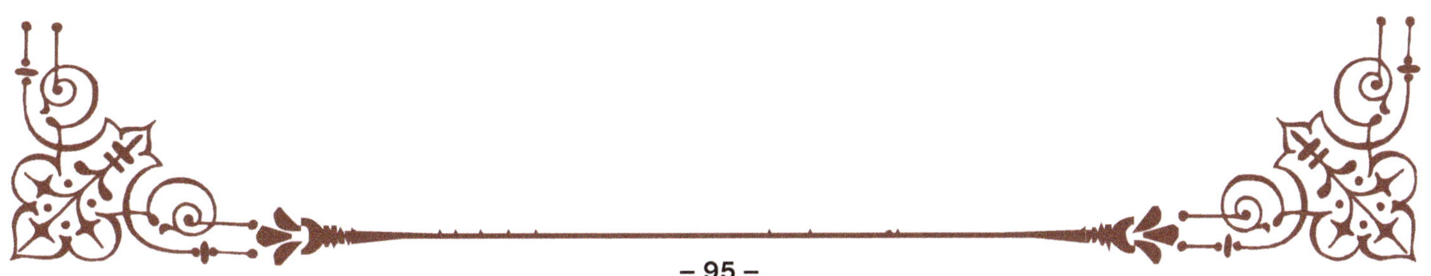

10 months of to and fro in words and demonstrations I still can't bare the fact that she doesn't understand that the passion which burns within desire the Presence of her embrace.

"10th Dollar."

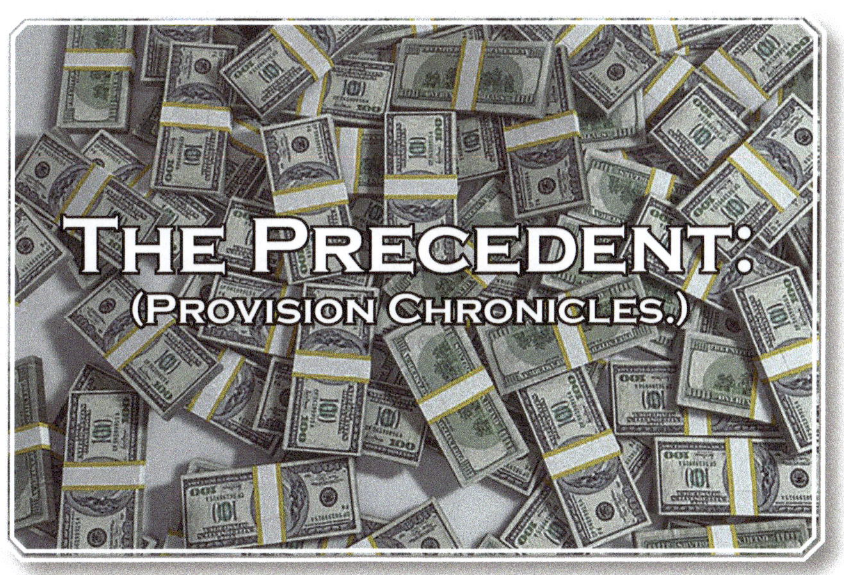
THE PRECEDENT:
(PROVISION CHRONICLES.)

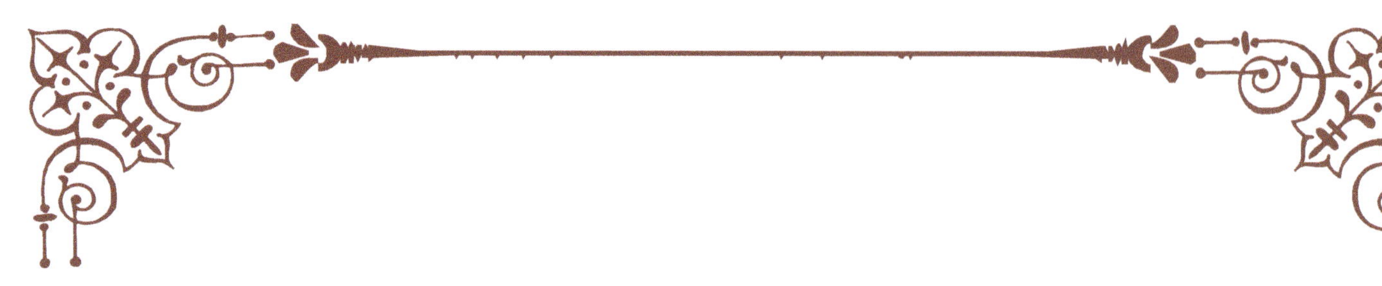

Always Love Donisha.

I would always love a woman which bring prestigious with the concept
for being a beautiful Black woman....."

"Always Love Donisha."

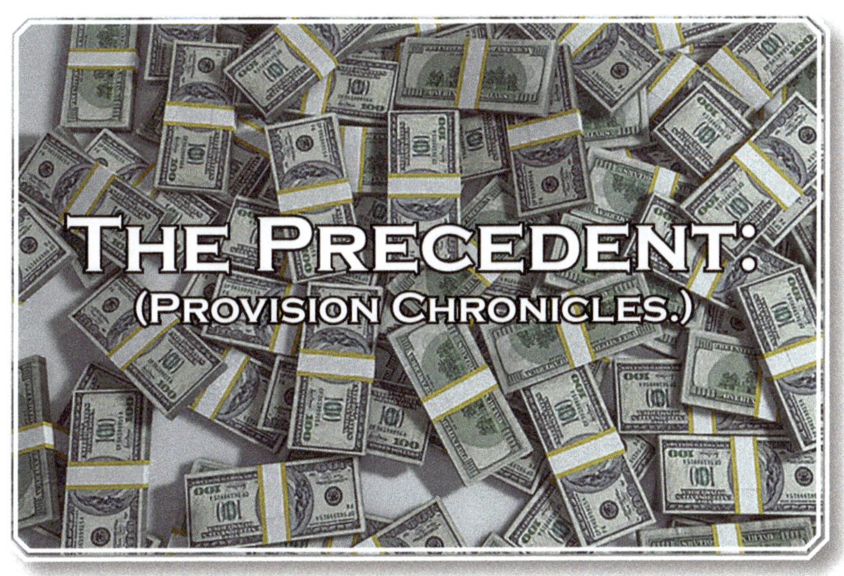

THE PRECEDENT:
(PROVISION CHRONICLES.)

Drummond Eats. II

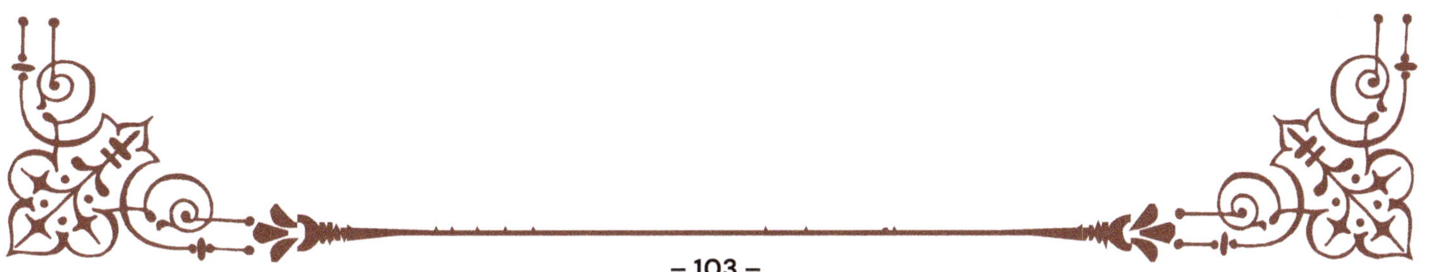

Deliberate but brief is what I'd seek for those to Understand.
When it comes time to partake of what is ours as we eat on the go.

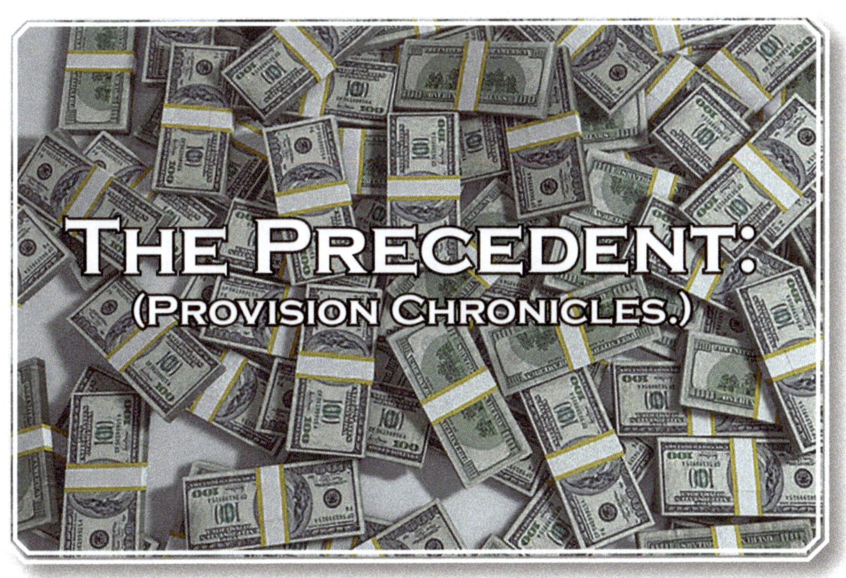

THE PRECEDENT:
(PROVISION CHRONICLES.)

Simple kind of Syka

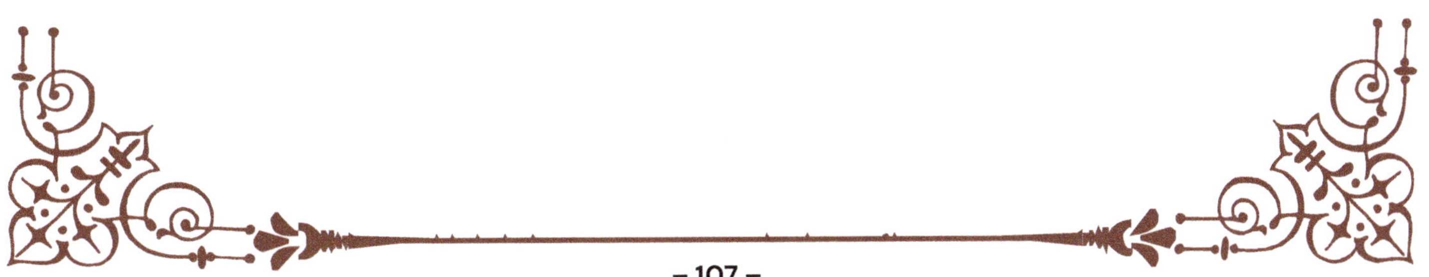

Syka divers from the origination of Jamaican music but keeps the oracles in rooted sound. Simple with a unique touch to an New breed founded within ska.

THE PRECEDENT:
(PROVISION CHRONICLES.)

GWEN GIRLS.

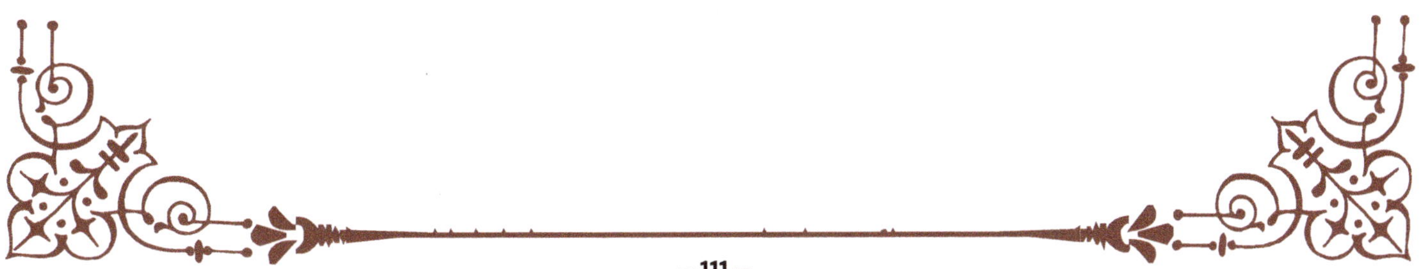

In the stability of privilege most women see it care free to wonder
about the Peace and civility of African People. We reach far beyond
will and deed to replace those who care less about us.

THE PRECEDENT:
(PROVISION CHRONICLES.)

Black Syka.

Black but Syka the ghetto isn't far fetch from the word but called "Black Syka."

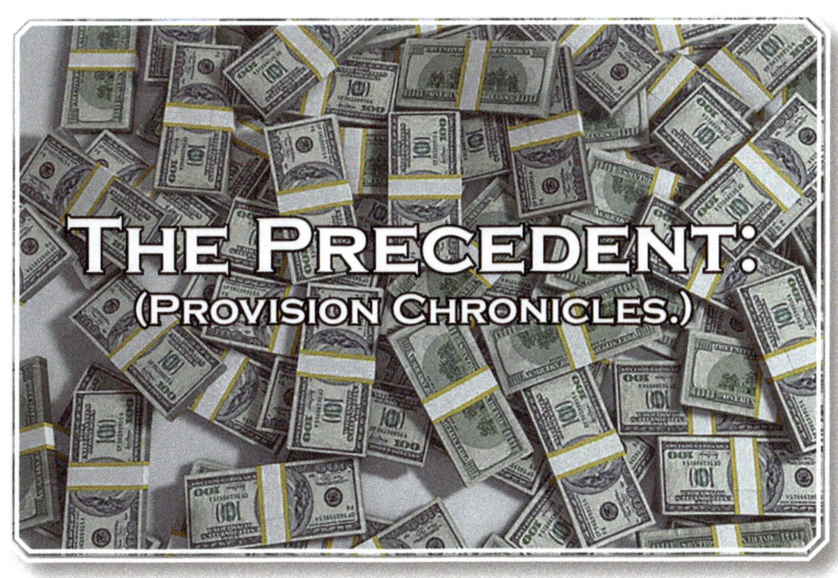
The Precedent:
(Provision Chronicles.)

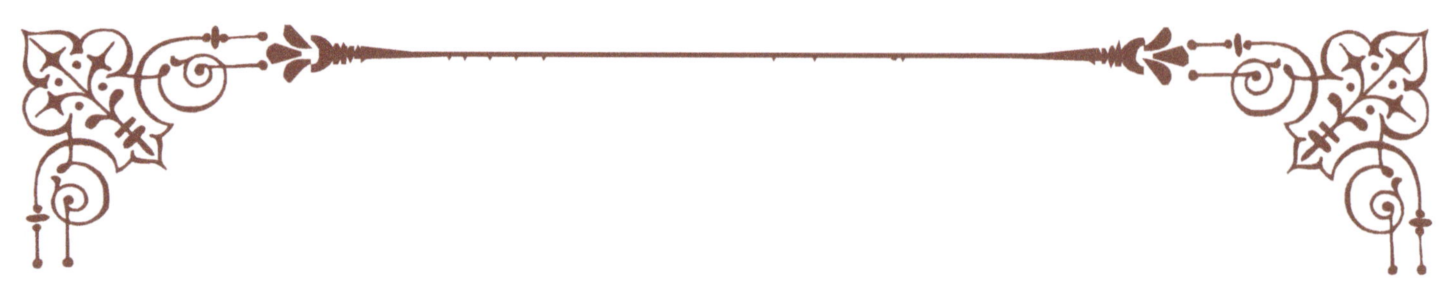

"Gunfest"

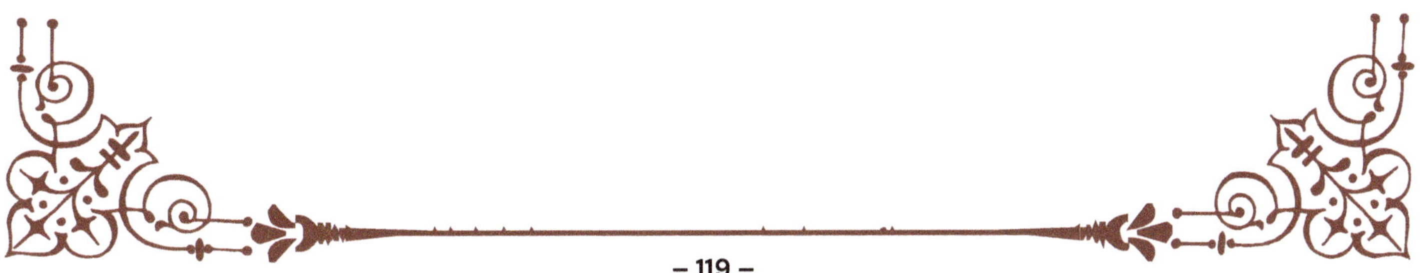

When that Police officer pulled a Gun on you I said this couldn't be
true……"

"Gunfest."

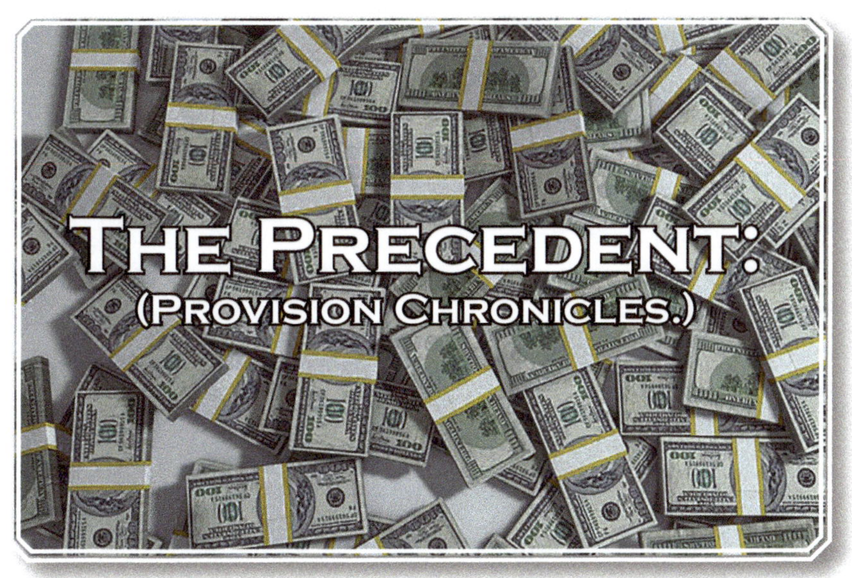

THE PRECEDENT:
(PROVISION CHRONICLES.)

OPEN
HOUSE

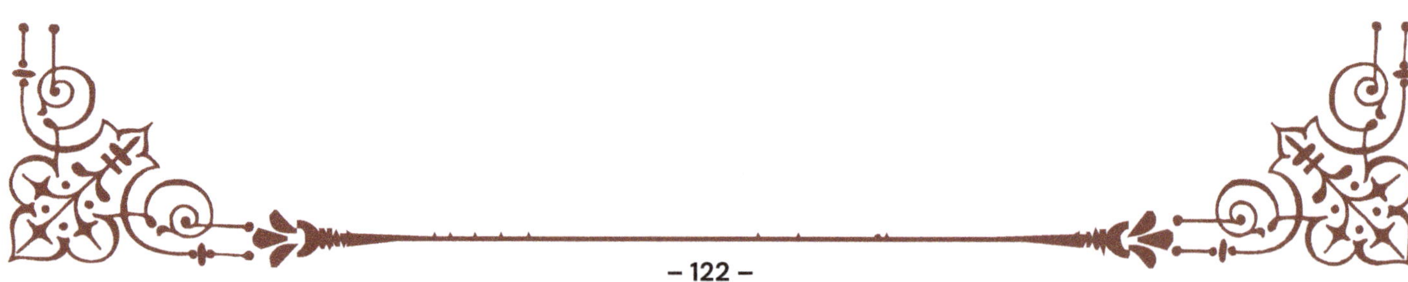

A sisterly sellout

Before you jeopardize the future wellbeing of my children; see it necessary not to salvage. The mere honor within Life to filthy rags of torn sackcloth. Pass down dishonor from a sisterly name that's a sellout.

THE PRECEDENT:
(PROVISION CHRONICLES.)

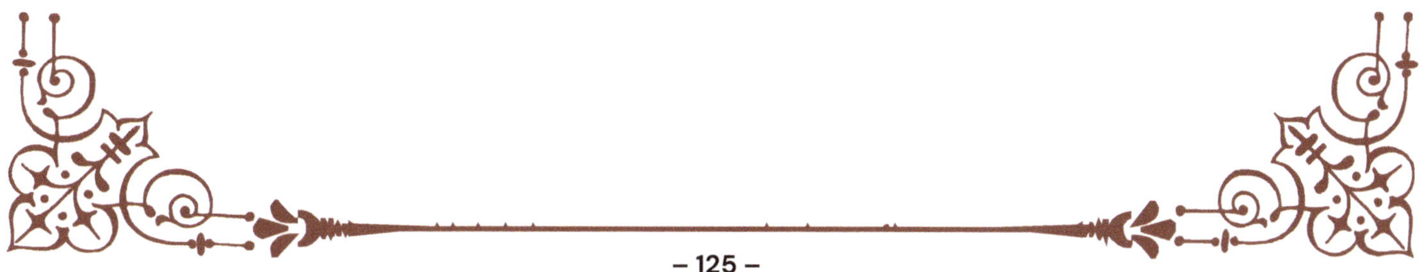

Assets & Accustom always.

Hidden from the admiration of onlookers who see it necessary to steal every earning for their self gain though I don't understand what they want Assets always accustomed.

THE PRECEDENT:
(PROVISION CHRONICLES.)

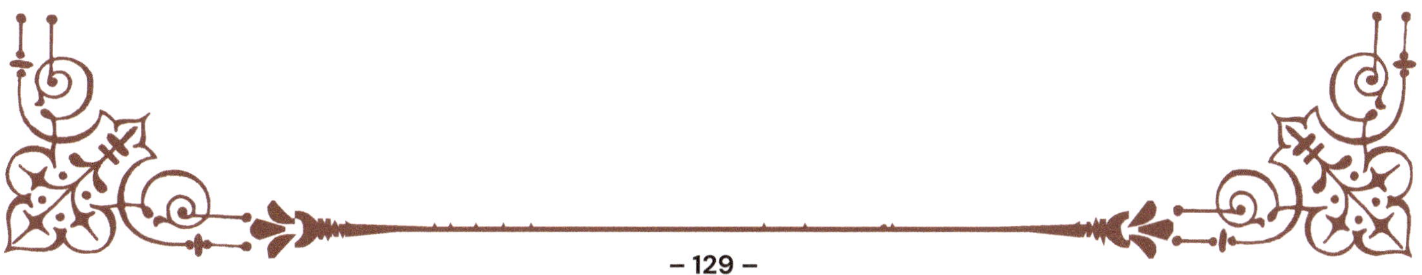

WHITE PANTHER.

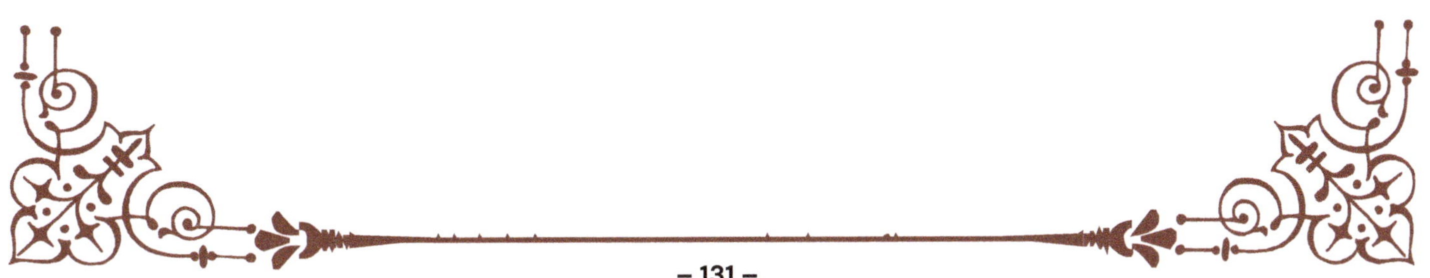

Even in White a Panther is honored as a reliable source of well watched Health and importance it is necessary to call it Royalty.

THE PRECEDENT:
(PROVISION CHRONICLES.)

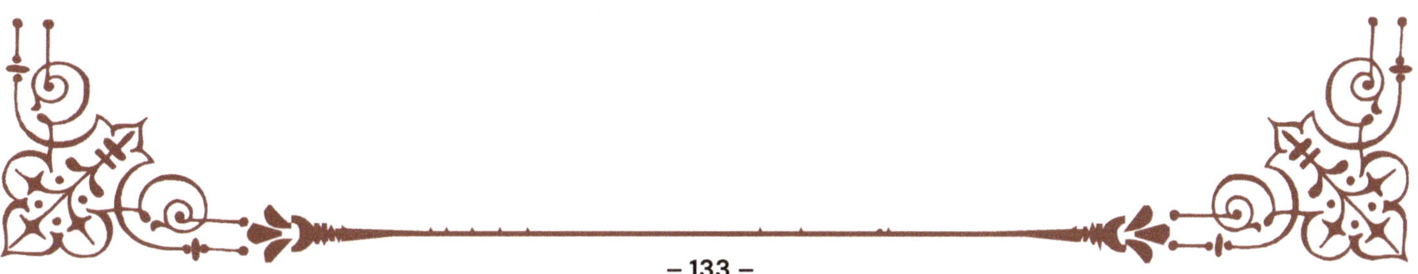

A Fatherly Failure.

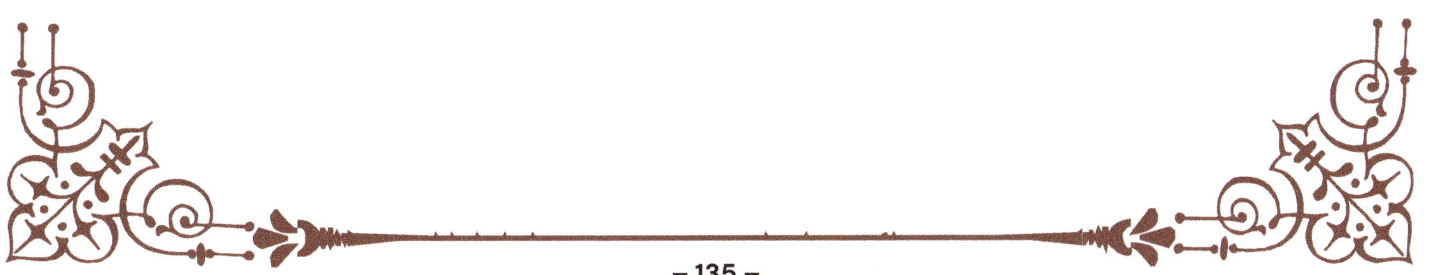

As a Father I haven't seen the strips of sacrifice; which a man teaches his son. Everything that I've learnt, anything that I've obtain. I did it through hard work fought in day and night seeking ways to uphold my success in Life. Now that I am a Man I don't need fatherly word to subject me to Failure.

THE PRECEDENT:
(PROVISION CHRONICLES.)

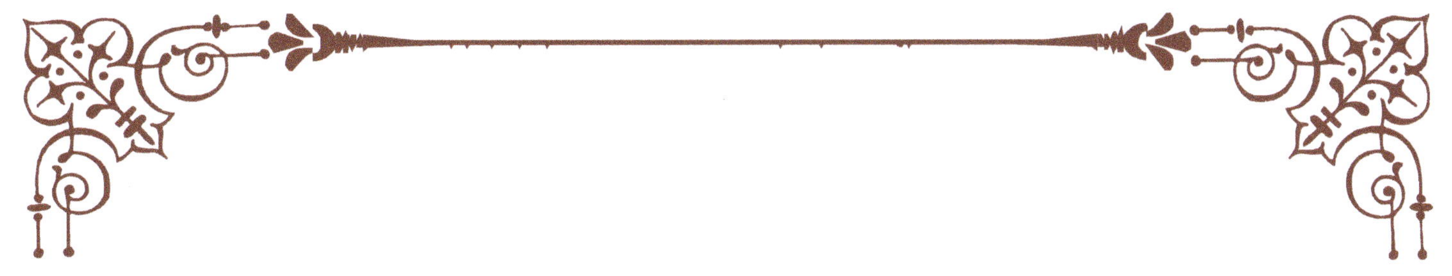

SYKGGAE.

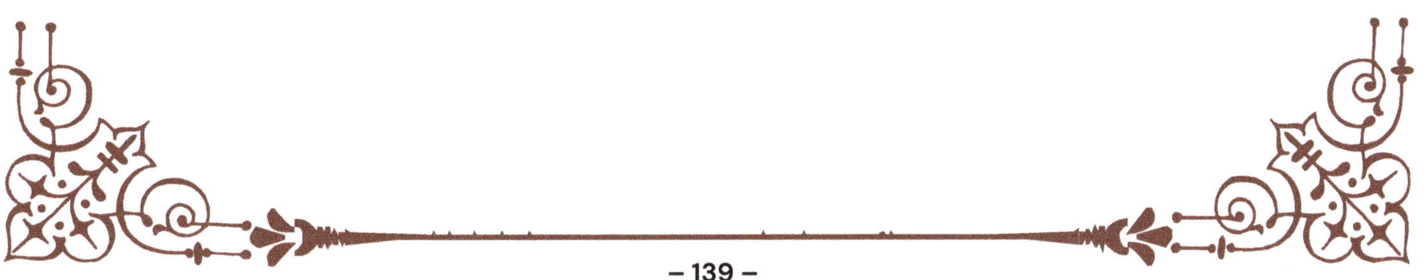

When Syka met Reggae they created Sykggae. A glamorous woman who provoke her Father Syka to jealousy. Though she made her mother Reggae smile, when she told her that was attracted to a guy name Jazz………"

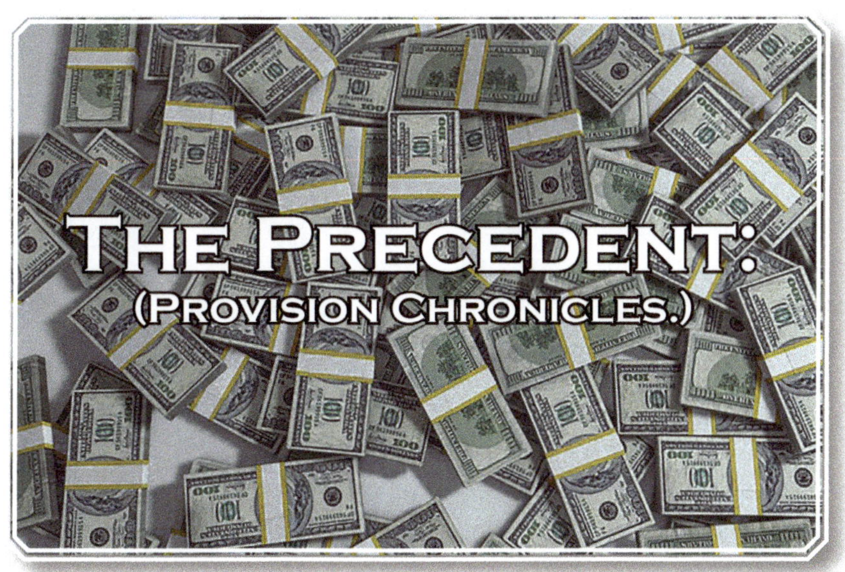
THE PRECEDENT:
(PROVISION CHRONICLES.)

The Robinson.

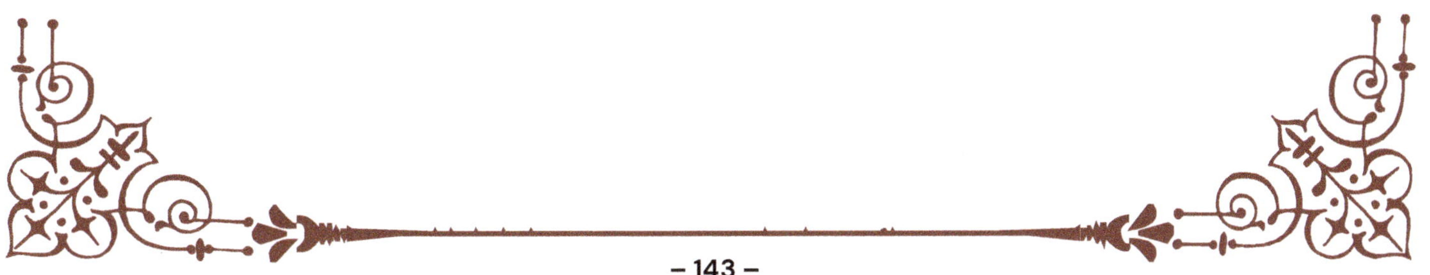

When looking at her picture I slowly start to see. The future for what
I want my daughter to be respectable, Intelligent, desirable towards
wanting to know more about a Life called "The Robinson."

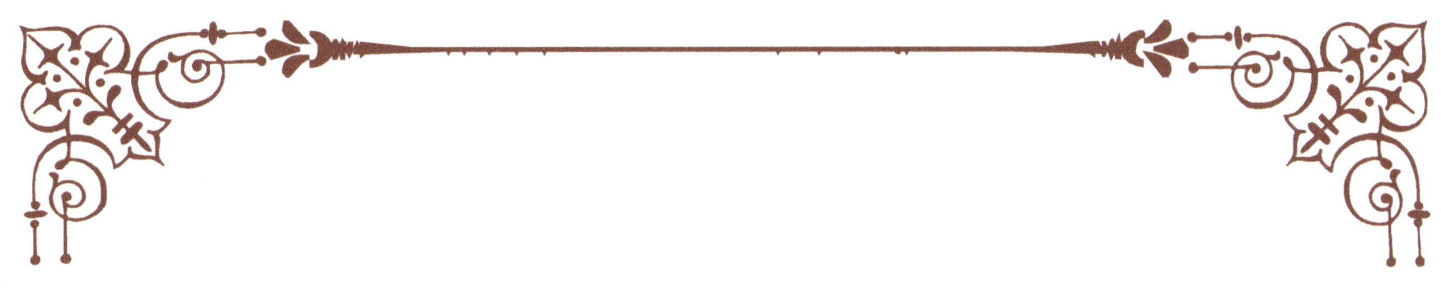

THE PRECEDENT:
(PROVISION CHRONICLES.)

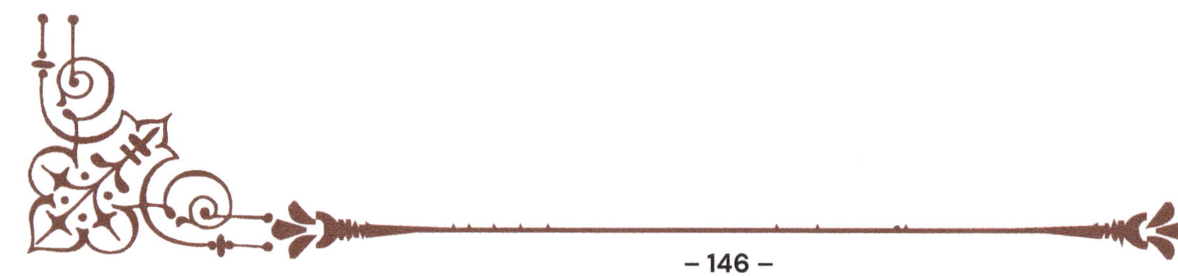

Nice & Drummond.

Nice but Drummond is impacted by verbal slander at the cost
of everything. Simple though hard to truly be with the one I love.
Deliberate even destructive that people don't understand that baring
of sacrifice in being who I am.

THE PRECEDENT:
(PROVISION CHRONICLES.)

Golden Guitar.

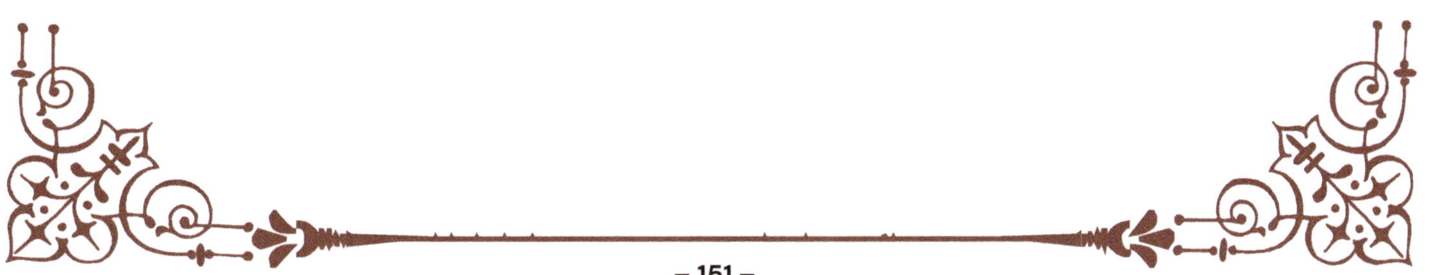

Golden but brass Guitar stringed with percussion and sounds which leads to the voice that play the tunes to these songs we call music.

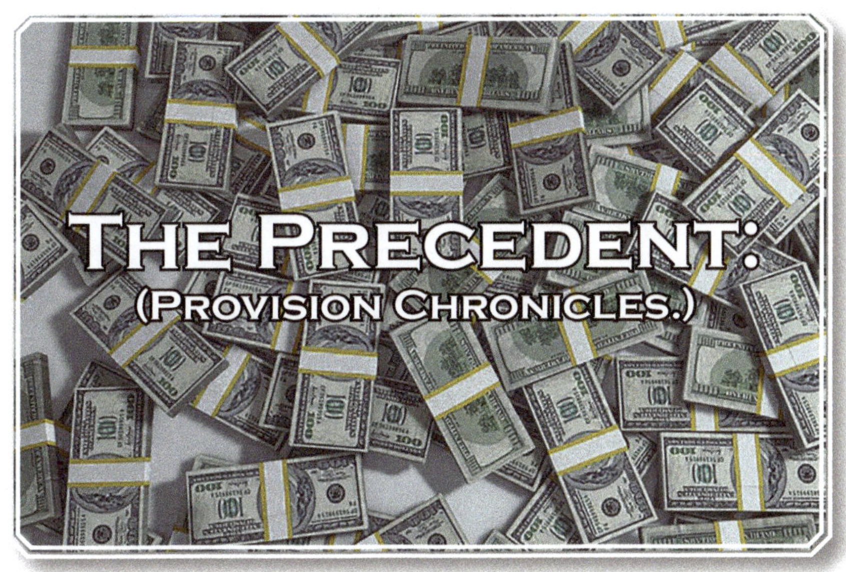
THE PRECEDENT:
(PROVISION CHRONICLES.)

The Aventura.

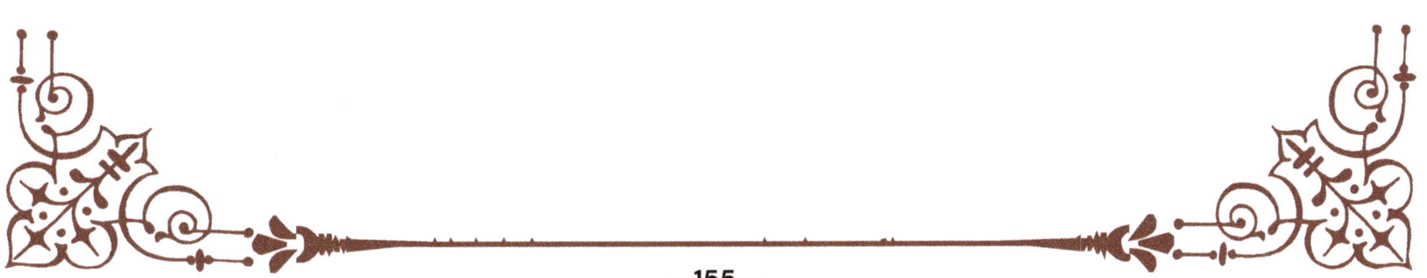

Even In Aventura walking through the mall I think about the whereabouts and concerns of a woman which activism exceeds the sounds for words to speak in contradiction toward her but love flow as rivers connecting Life and Rastafari.

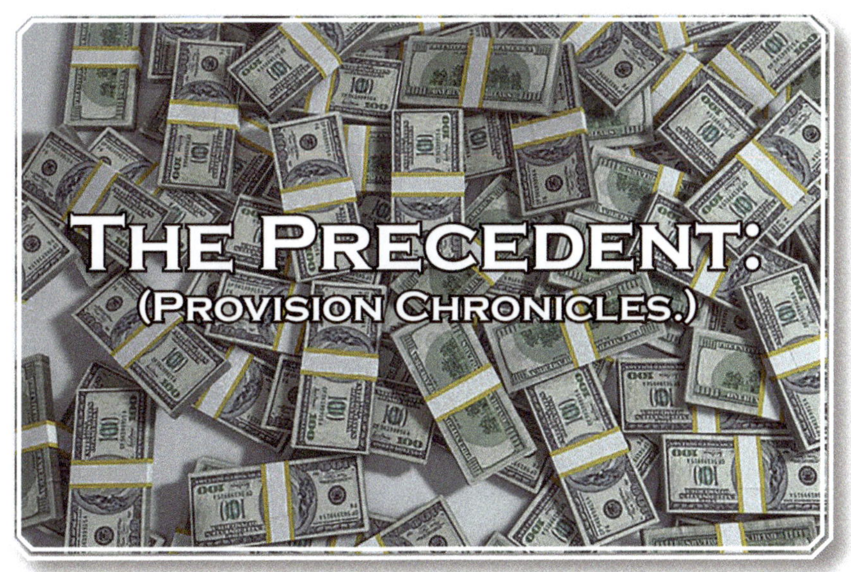

THE PRECEDENT:
(PROVISION CHRONICLES.)

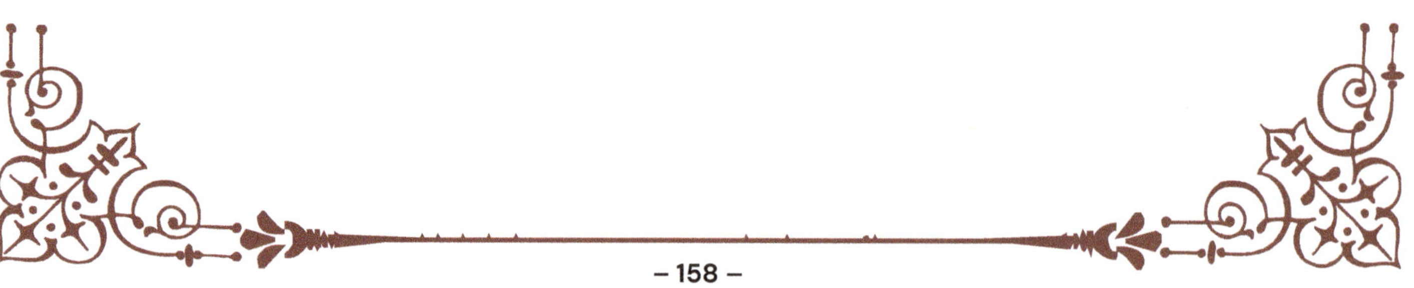

KILL THE SIG.

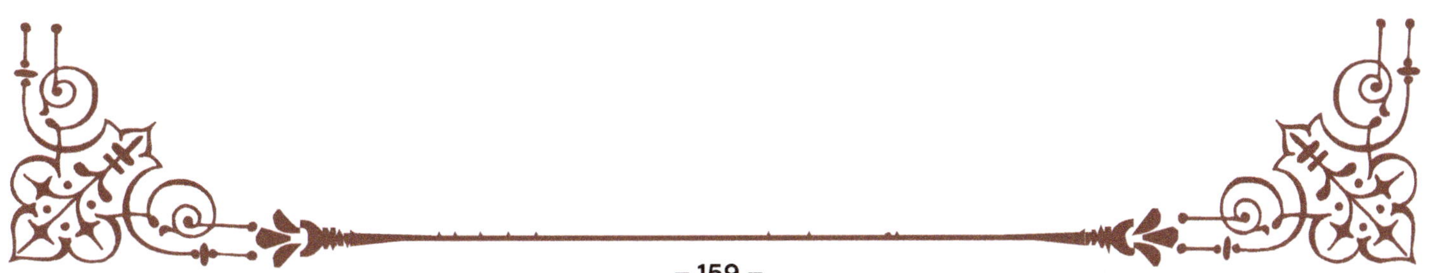

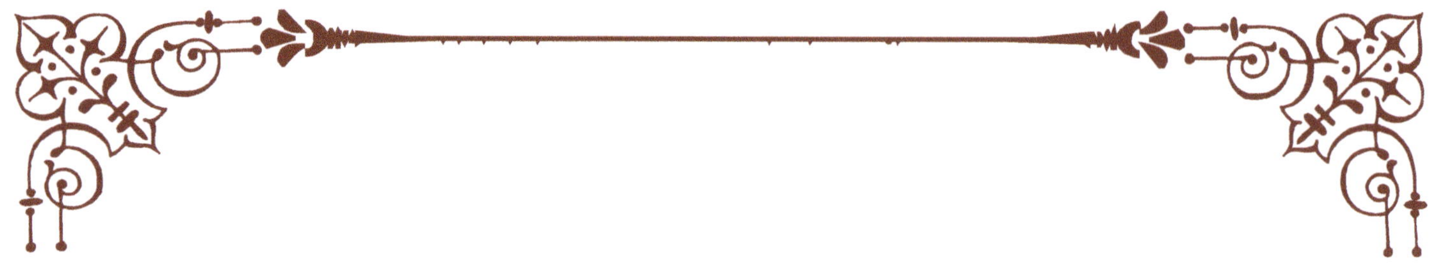

Kill the mystic of corruption which dethrone the reality for Peace we speak from the strength in Realization to "kill the sig."

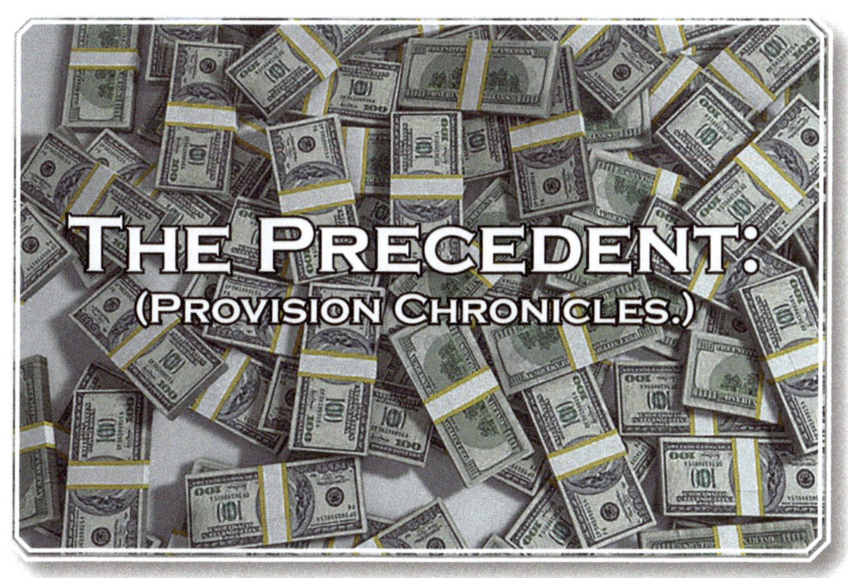
THE PRECEDENT:
(PROVISION CHRONICLES.)

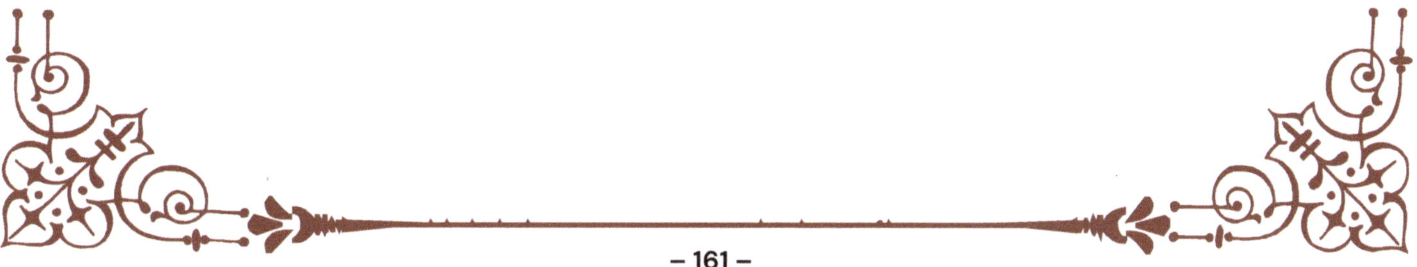

King of the Drummond

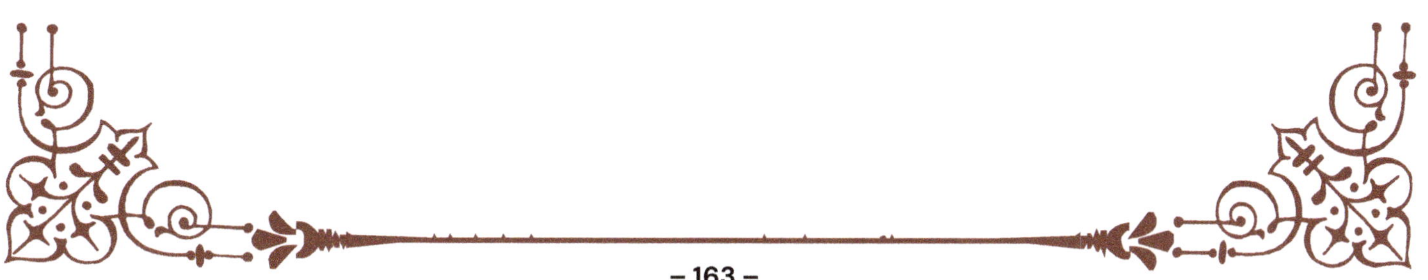

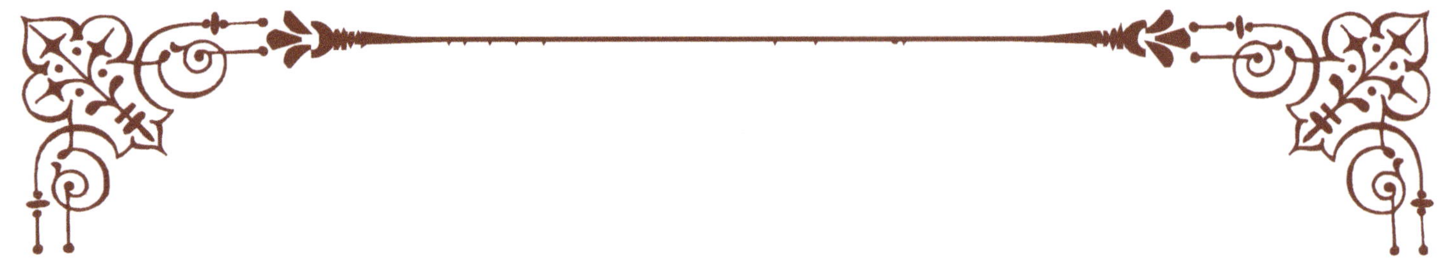

I am not the King of the original Drummond from ska Music but a
entailed description from what is New in the Heart of Kings who see a
newer arising……"

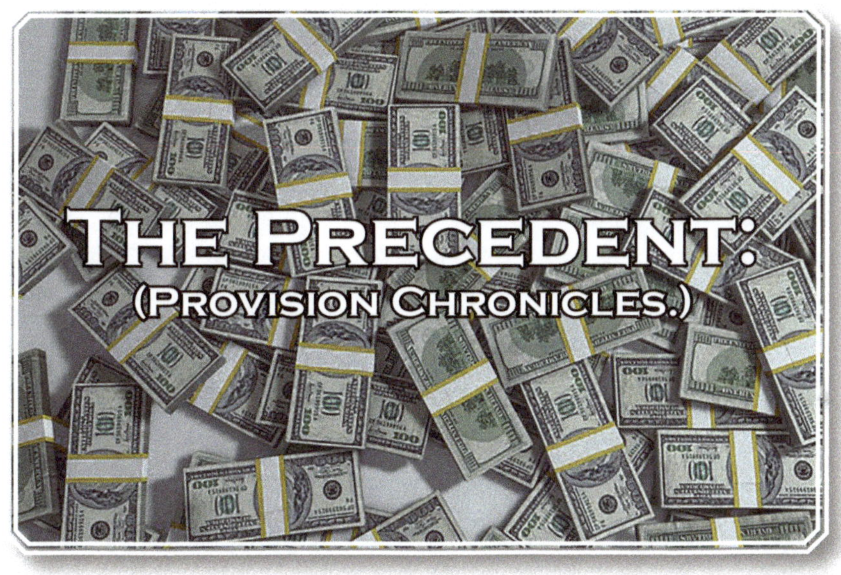

THE PRECEDENT:
(PROVISION CHRONICLES.)

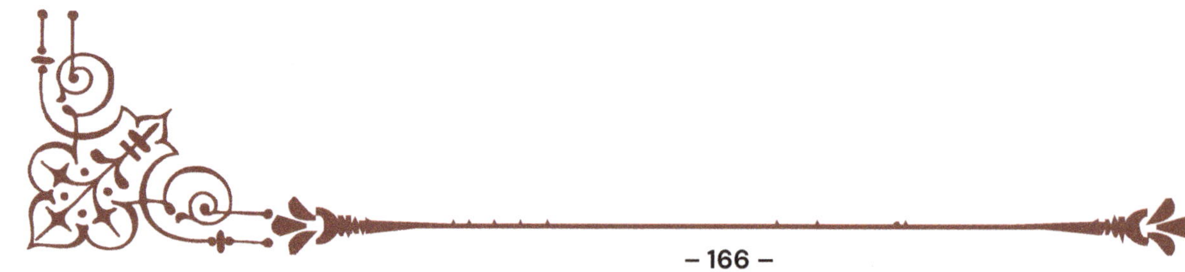

DANCEFEST.

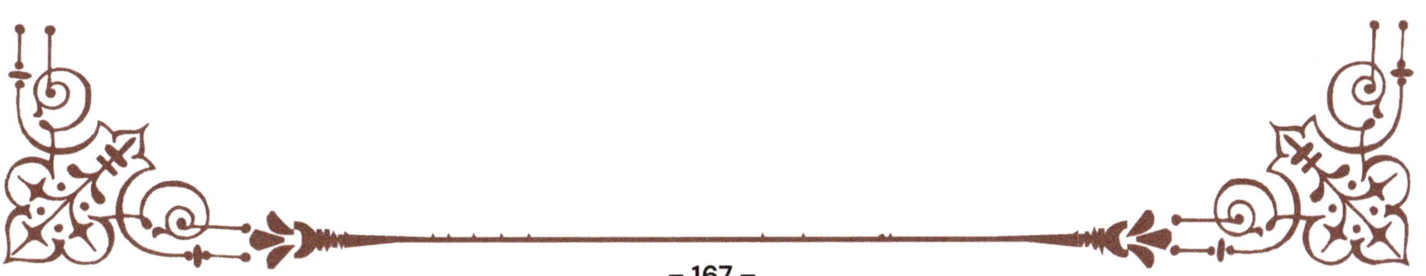

Dancefest is the celebration of Dancehall music which touches both Hardcore and New age Dancehall representing Music from all genres bringing to reality Jamaican culture.

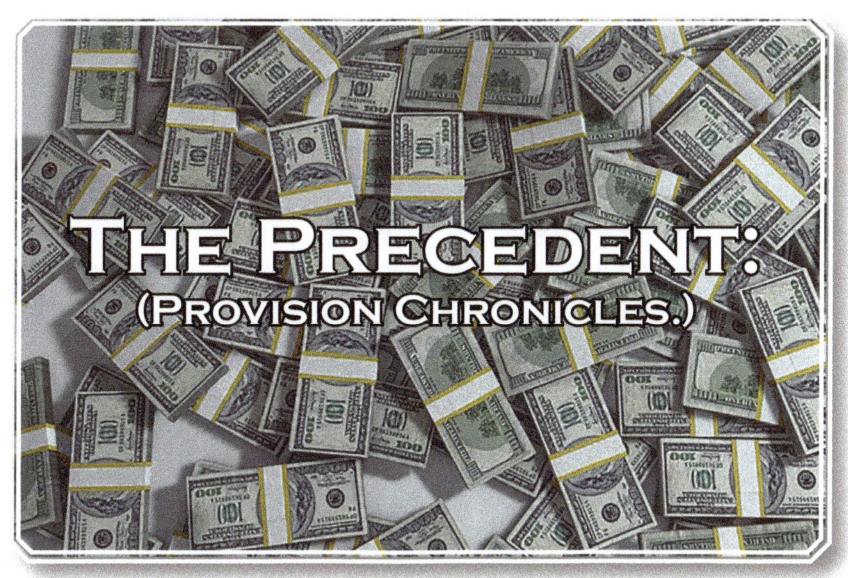
THE PRECEDENT:
(PROVISION CHRONICLES.)

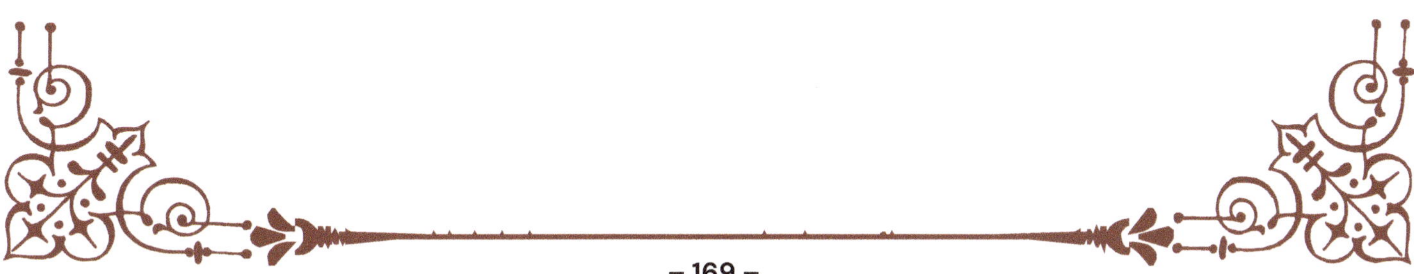

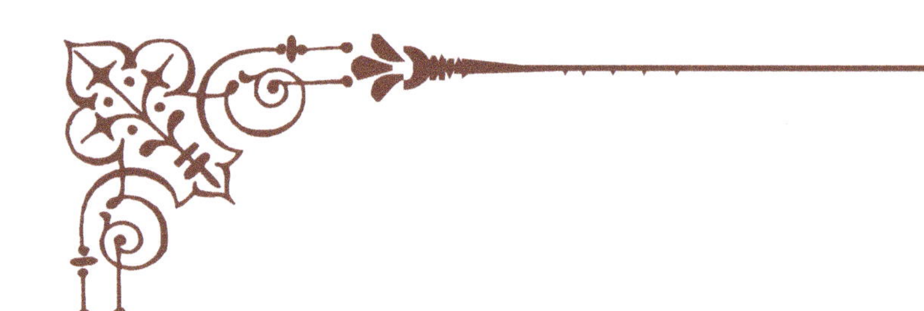

Barack Obama Blvd. II

Even in Florida where the streets aren't always subjected to public demonstration somewhere there is a place called
"Barack Obama Blvd."

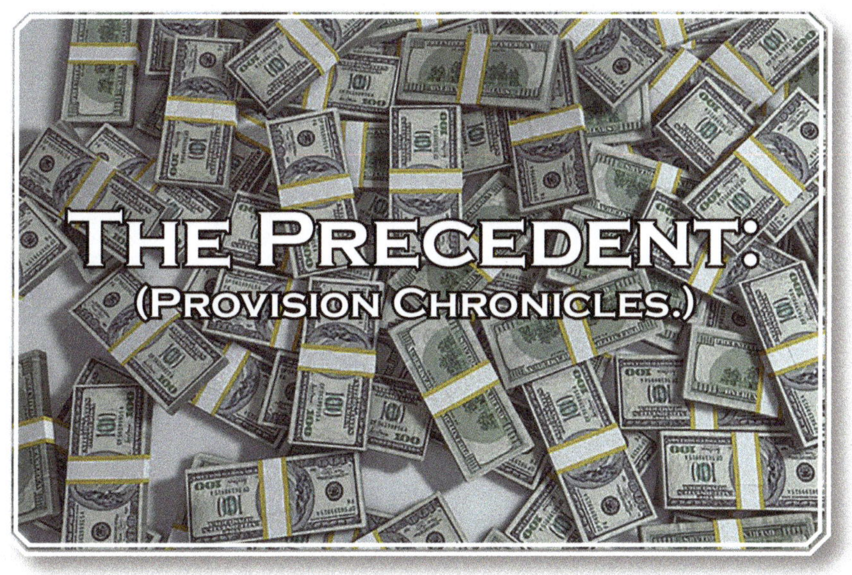
THE PRECEDENT:
(PROVISION CHRONICLES.)

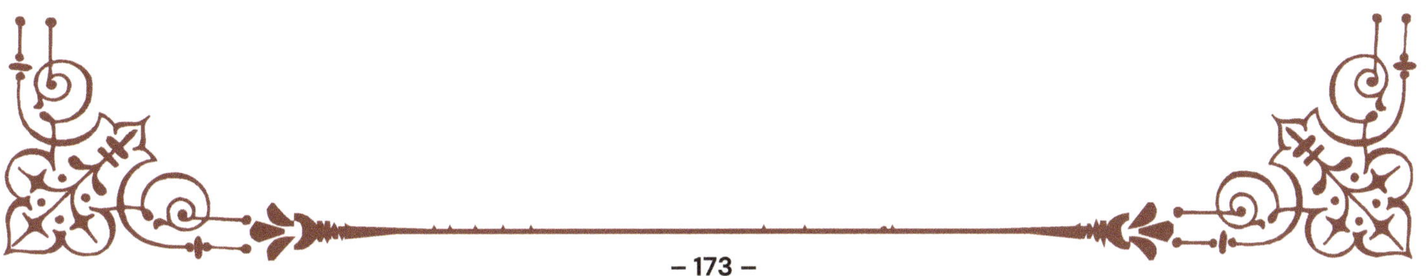

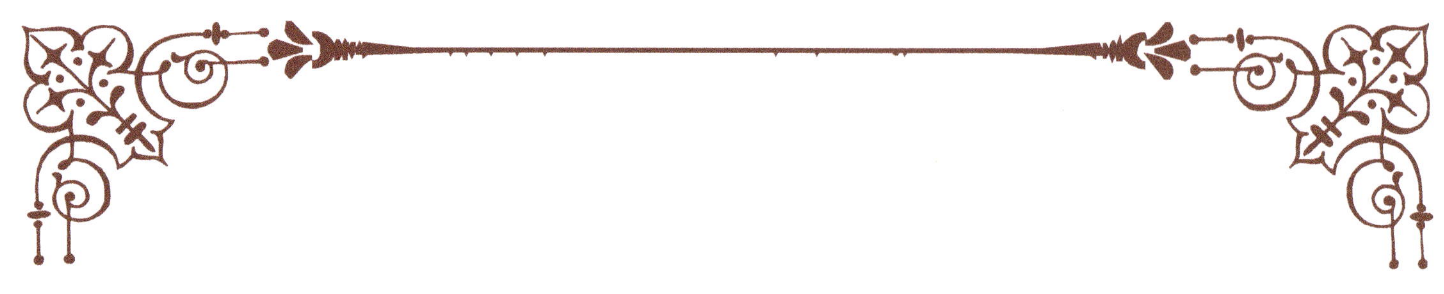

Nothing with Drummond.

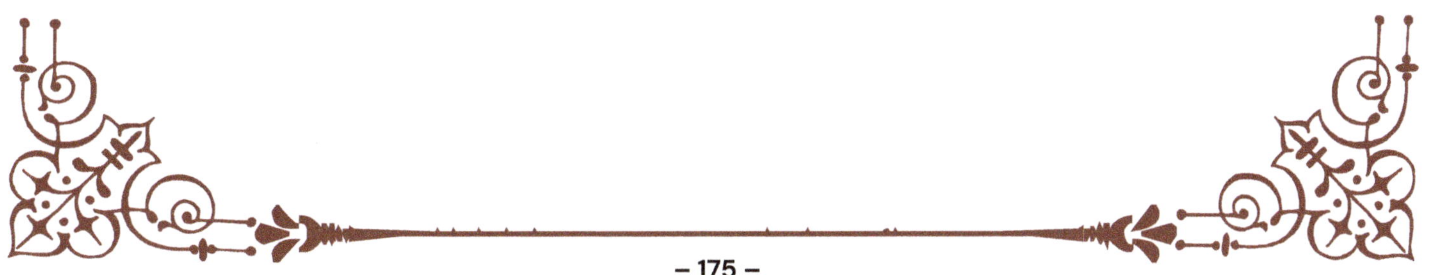

Nothing with those who are Drummond but use their voice to degrade and verbally abuse those who they call relatives. Always make it seem that their belief in suggestion is right no matter the cost towards negativity.

THE PRECEDENT:
(PROVISION CHRONICLES.)

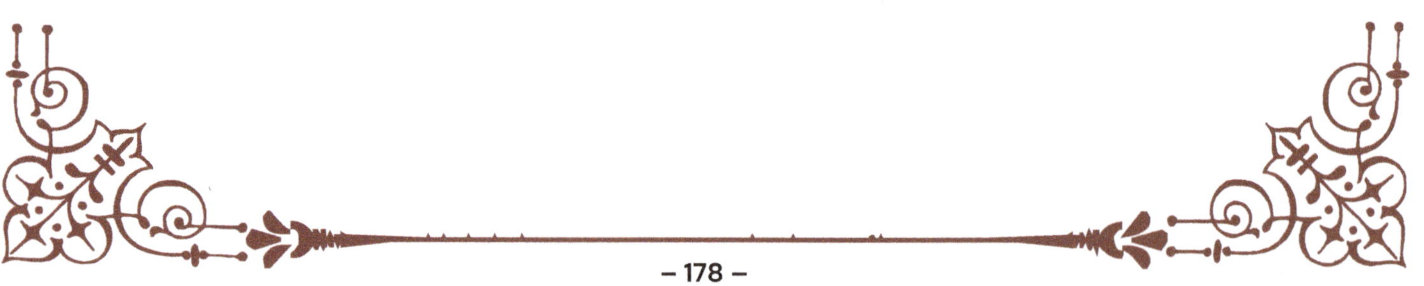

MARY.

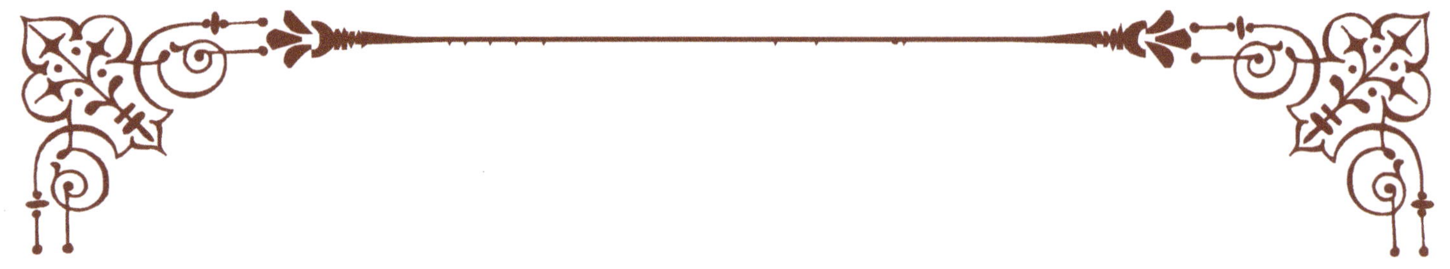

Black but beautiful your words touches the most inner depths of emptiness. Through passion and envy from who you are desire seeketh evermore grateful for "Mary."

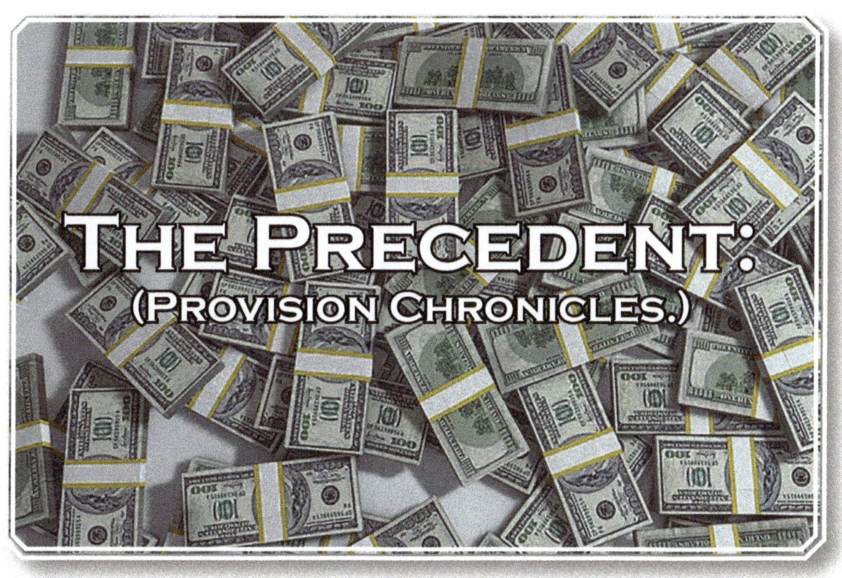

THE PRECEDENT:
(PROVISION CHRONICLES.)

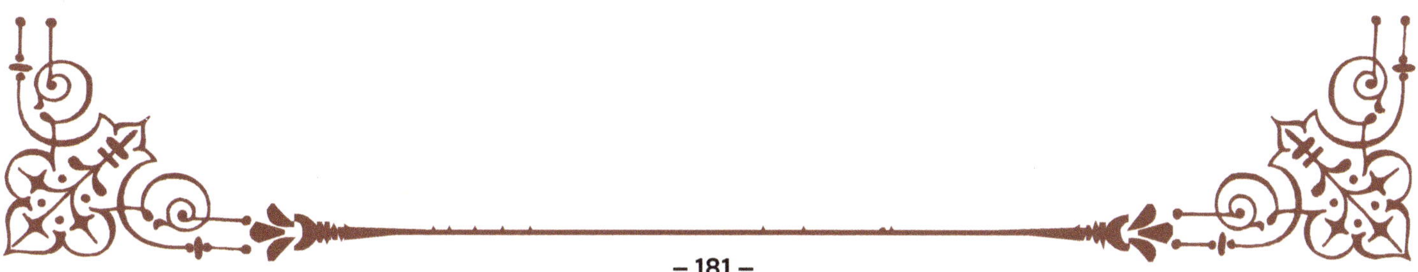

Drakeland. II

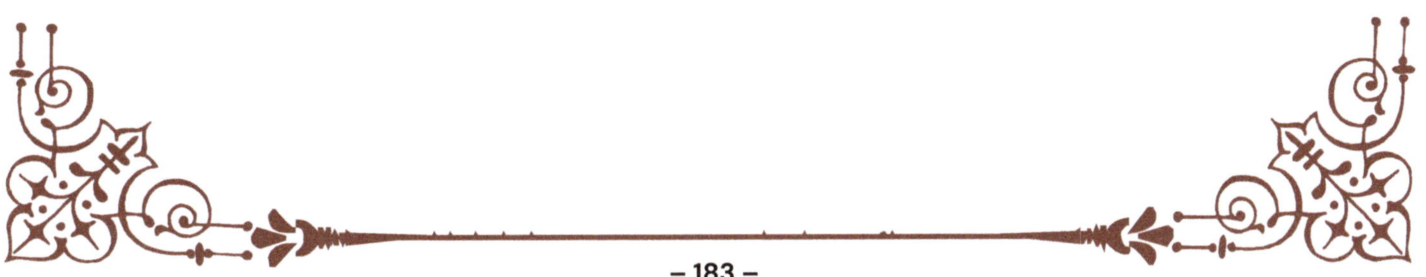

Even in Jamaica foreigners come in and steal the Music that we love
so dearly Reggae Music.......”

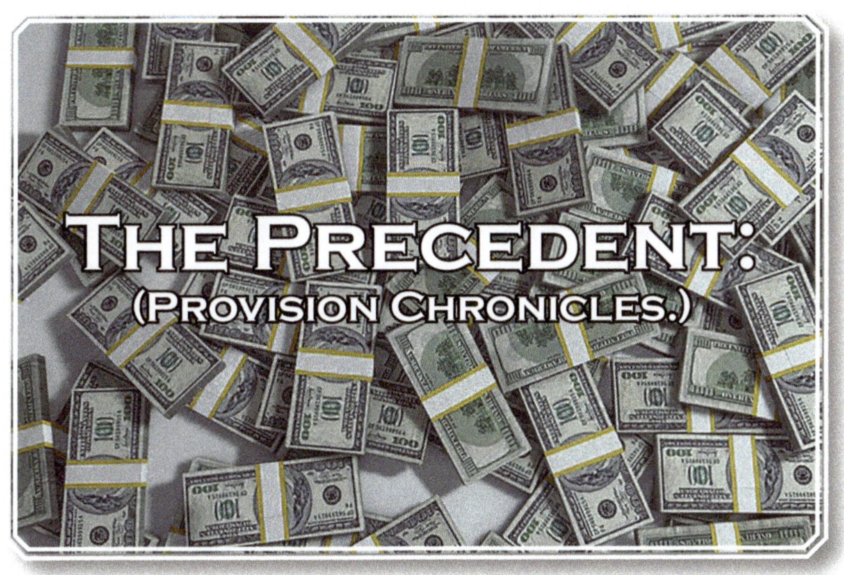
THE PRECEDENT:
(PROVISION CHRONICLES.)

Ownfest.

Even in ownership the reward of greatness should always exceed the
reality for festive impartiality.

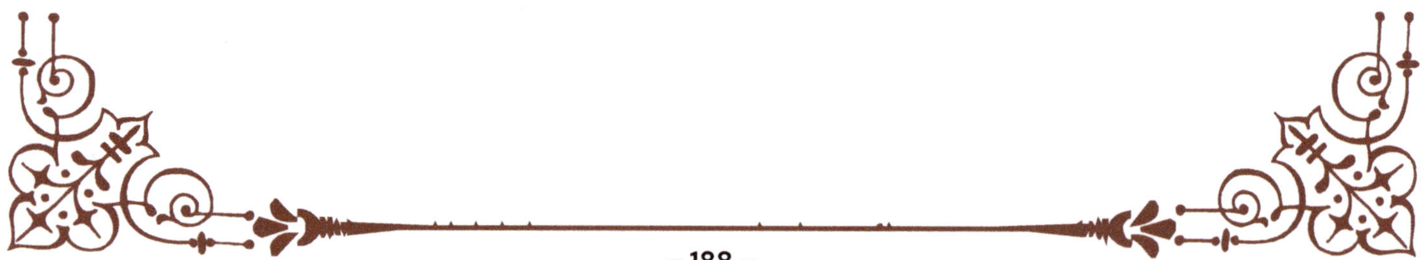

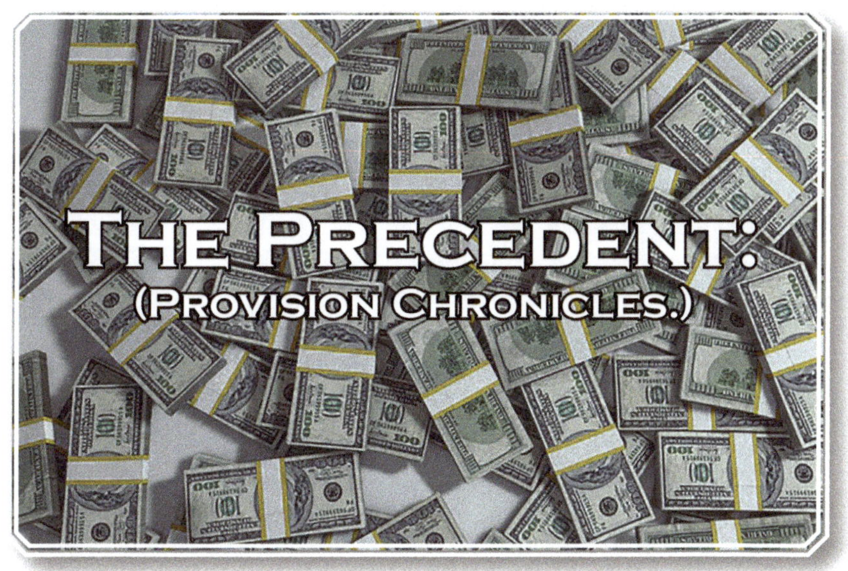

THE PRECEDENT:
(PROVISION CHRONICLES.)

DRUMMOND NOT GHETTO.

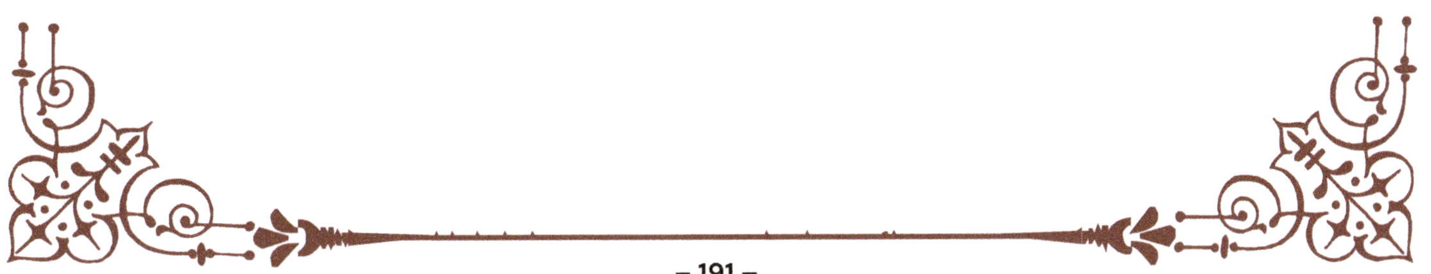

Drummond relates to the Ghetto were crime highly proceeds the will for change but Peace is always in need where Love is.

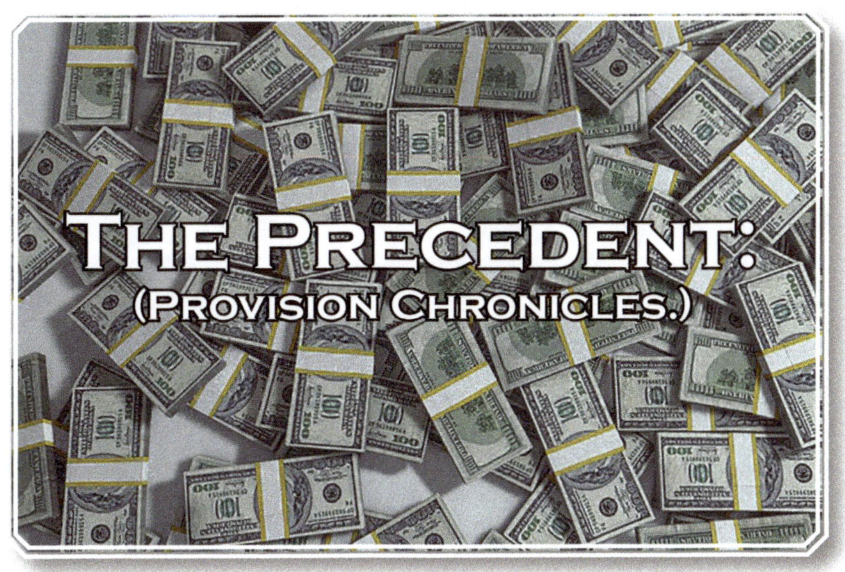
The Precedent:
(Provision Chronicles.)

Bentley Truck.

A highly priced concealed by gasoline that pushes up the status quo
of what we call America from the standard called a Bentley truck.
Which uses the price of entailed exploitation to cause
People to give Dollars.

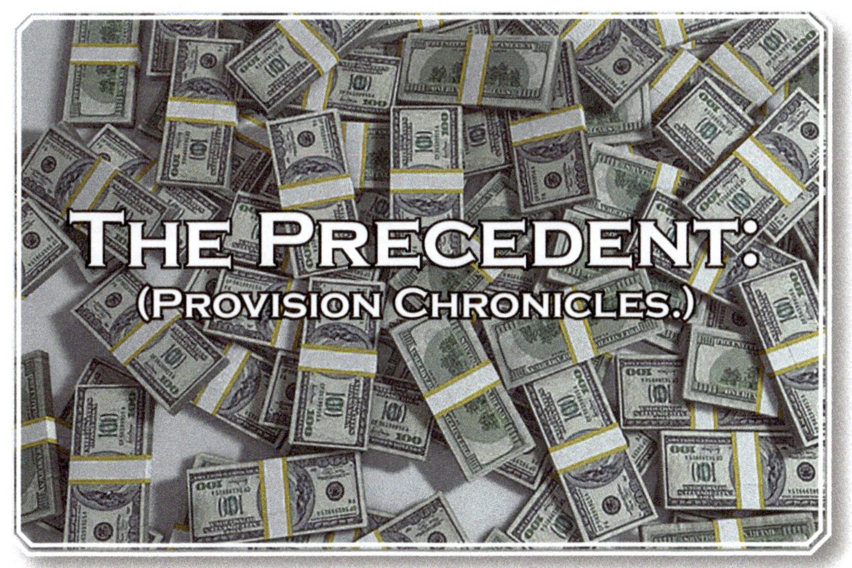

THE PRECEDENT:
(PROVISION CHRONICLES.)

Drummond not Secrets

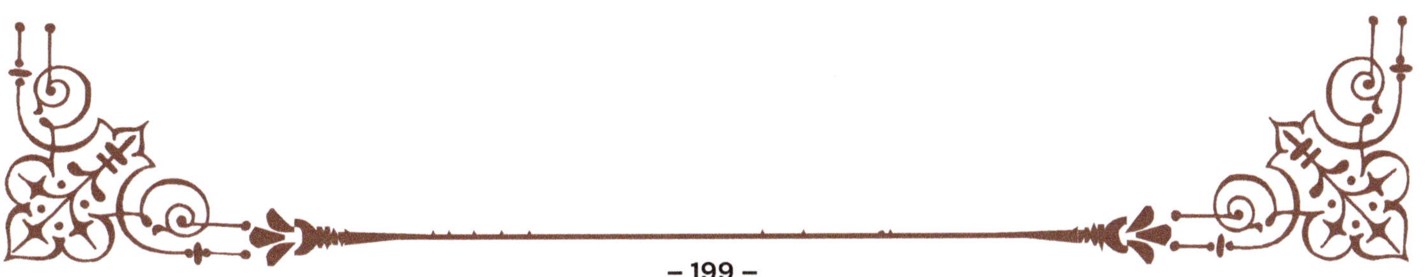

Drummond is Privately secretive but publicly open to whatever should
be necessary toward Life inward change from Pain.

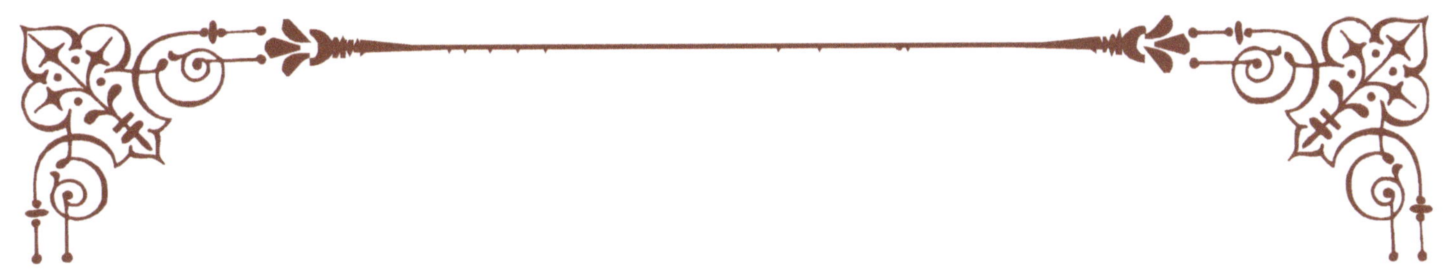

THE PRECEDENT:
(PROVISION CHRONICLES.)

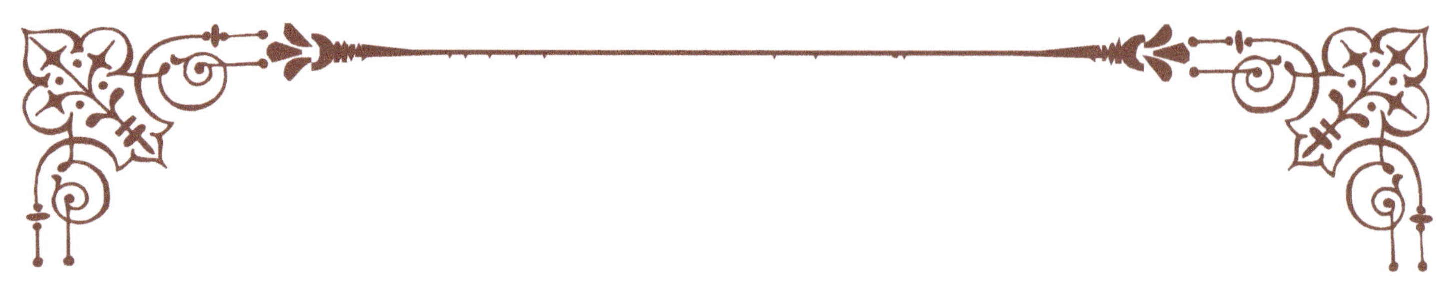

STILL LOVE DONISHA.

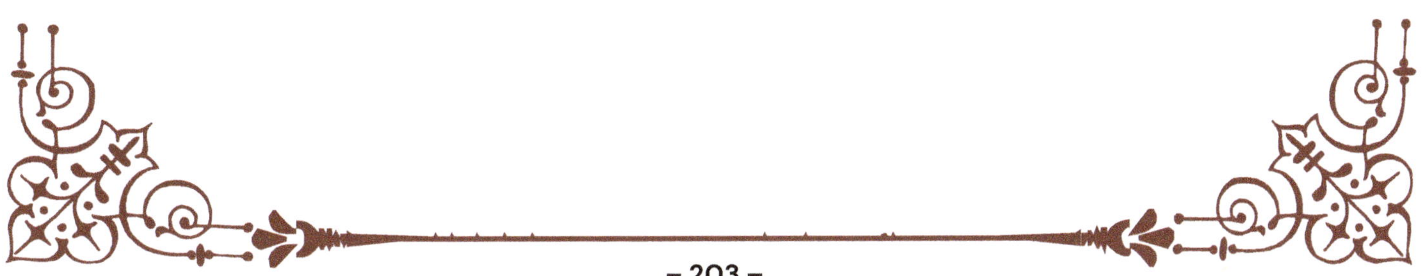

Even In admiration I start to wonder about the daily sacrifices which captures her beauty. Still I start to think about every flaw which lies in me. Though I haven't began to Understand that Life isn't what you want it to be just where it supposed to go.

"Still Love Donisha."

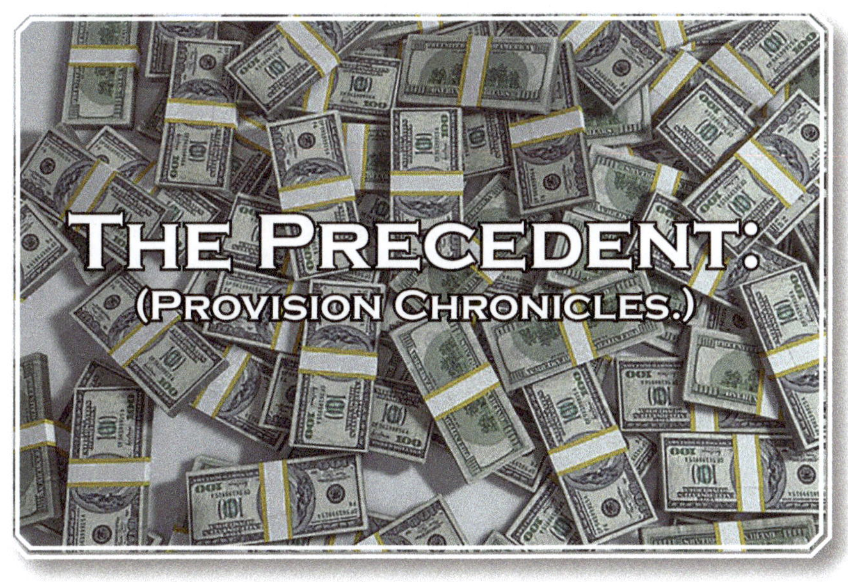

THE PRECEDENT:
(PROVISION CHRONICLES.)

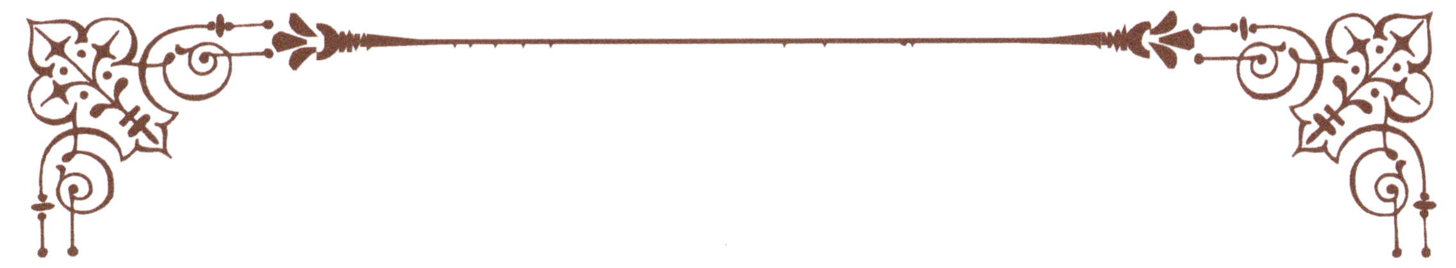

PRENDERGAST NOT PERISH.

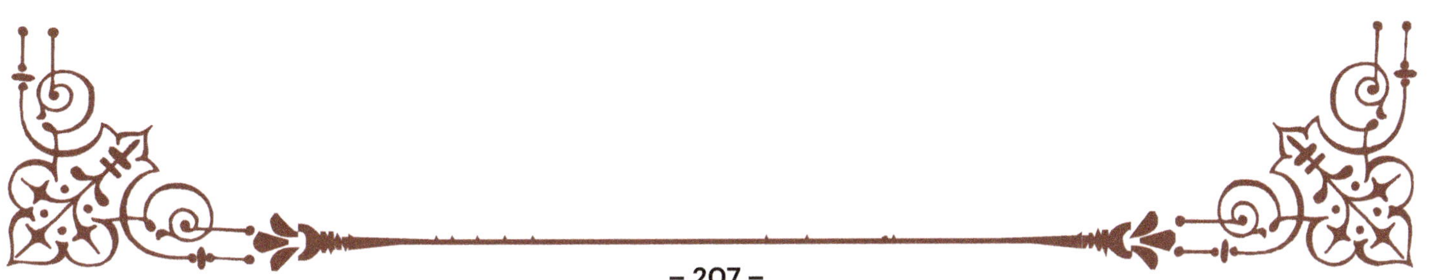

We must respect each other as People regardless of any circumstance. We must hold dare the fragility of women even if we don't understand. We must also believe that Love is stronger that any material gain made to separate us from those who Love us.

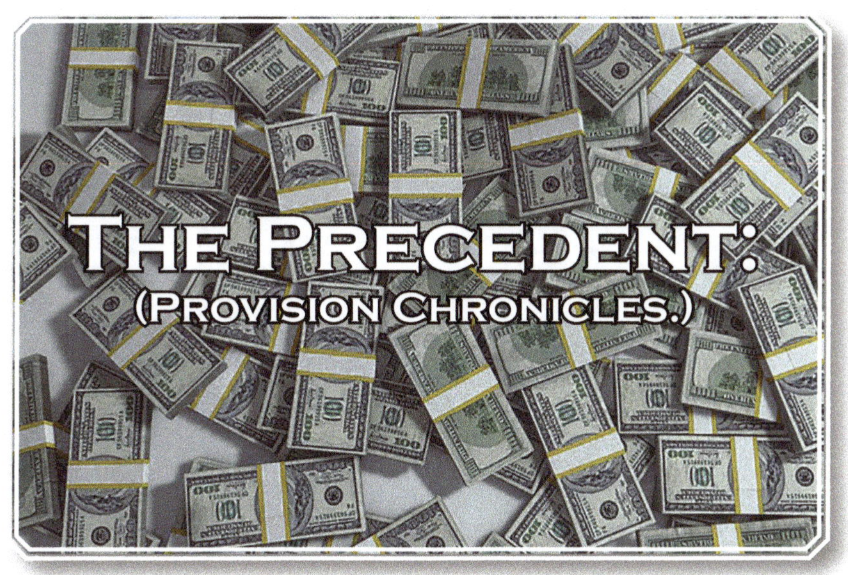

THE PRECEDENT:
(PROVISION CHRONICLES.)

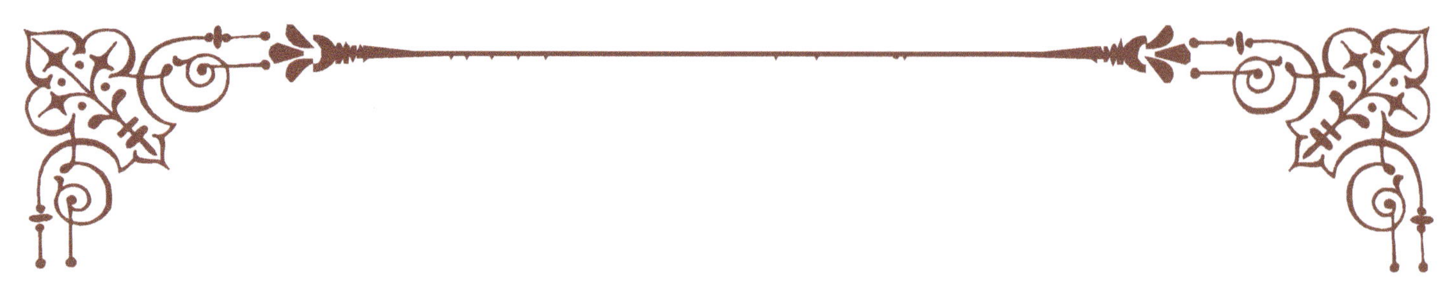

THE PRECEDENT:
(PROVISION CHRONICLES.)

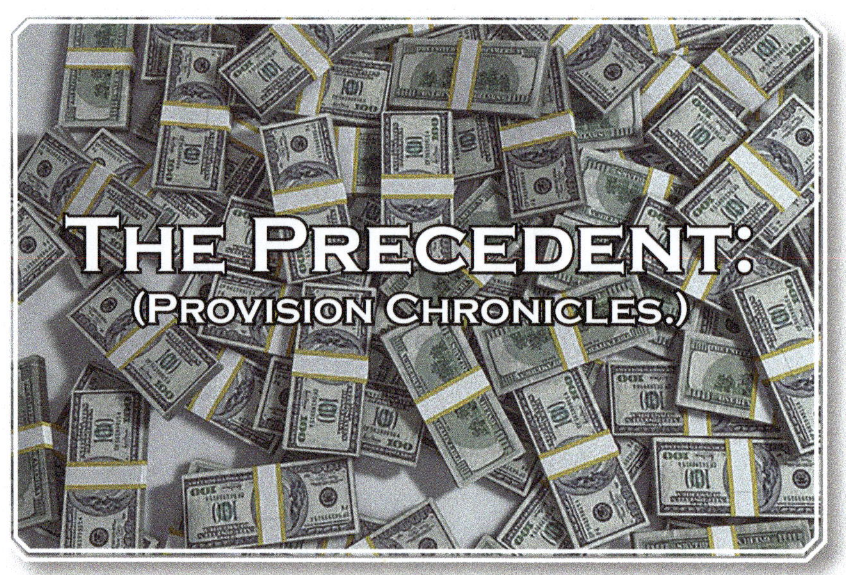

ACKNOWLEDGMENTS

I would like to first thank God for blessing me with the gift of Poetry.
Secondly I want to thank my Mother for being there.
Lastly I appreciate everyone that contributed to this Book.

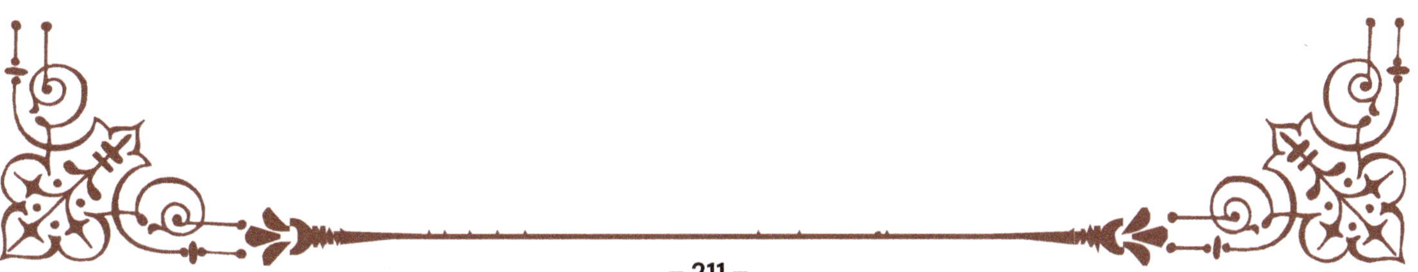